W9-AFC-502

DATE DUE

MAR 27 2014			

Emotion and Stress

GRAY
MATTER

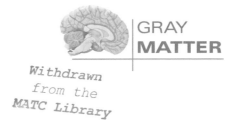

Emotion and Stress

F. Fay Evans-Martin, Ph.D.

Series Editor
Eric H. Chudler, Ph.D.

CHELSEA HOUSE
PUBLISHERS
An imprint of Infobase Publishing

With gratitude to Dr. Brad Bunnell,
With love to Shawn and Eric,
With honor to my loving Creator

Emotion and Stress

Copyright © 2007 by Infobase Publishing

Chelsea House
An imprint of Infobase Publishing
132 West 31st Street
New York NY 10001

Library of Congress Cataloging-in-Publication Data

Evans-Martin, F. Fay.
 Emotion and stress / F. Fay Evans-Martin.
    p. cm. — (Gray matter)
 Includes bibliographical references and index.
 ISBN-13: 978-0-7910-9491-4 (hardcover)
 ISBN-10: 0-7910-9491-X (hardcover)
 1. Emotions—Physiological aspects. 2. Stress (Psychology) 3. Stress(Physiology)
I. Title. II. Series.
 RC531.E93 2007
 616.001'9—dc22   2006101334

Chelsea House books are available at special discounts when purchased in bulk quantities for businesses, associations, institutions, or sales promotions. Please call our Special Sales Department in New York at (212) 967-8800 or (800) 322-8755.

You can find Chelsea House on the World Wide Web at http://www.chelseahouse.com

Text and cover design by Terry Mallon

Printed in the United States of America

Bang EJB 10 9 8 7 6 5 4 3 2 1

This book is printed on acid-free paper.

All links and Web addresses were checked and verified to be correct at the time of publication. Because of the dynamic nature of the Web, some addresses and links may have changed since publication and may no longer be valid.

Contents

1 | A Universal Language

Jonathan propped the end of his fishing pole against the riverbank and lay back in the grass to stare up at the fluffy clouds in the sky overhead. His eyes wandered to the tree branches nearby, where he spotted a squirrel busily eating its food. His sigh of contentment was abruptly interrupted as he heard a rustle in the brush behind him. Recent talk of bear sightings in the area flashed through his mind as his muscles tensed and his heart pounded. Almost afraid to move, he slowly rolled over to get a better view. He was flooded with relief as he saw his collie, Dandy, emerge from the bushes. Dandy rushed forward with a display of affection that made Jonathan laugh in pleasure as the two rolled in play on the grassy riverbank.

Back in the city, Jonathan's sister Jane arrived on the first floor of the building in which she was to interview for her first job with just minutes to spare. Traffic had been congested, and parking had been difficult. As she approached the elevators, she noticed that one was out of order and the other had apparently stopped several floors up. As she clutched her briefcase tightly, she contemplated walking up 15 flights of stairs but realized that she could never make it on time. Finally, the elevator doors opened in front of her, and she dashed through them and frantically pushed the button for the fifteenth floor. A number of other passengers were on board, and the elevator stopped several times on the way up to let them off and to let others on. By this time, Jane's heart was pounding, perspiration beaded her brow, and her hands were trembling. As the doors opened to the fifteenth floor, she rushed out and down the hall to the office where her interview was to be held. Jane nervously looked at her watch as she opened the door and approached the secretary's desk…. Just on time!

EMOTION AND STRESS

Emotions and stress are an important part of our daily lives. They definitely make life more interesting and challenging, but they also have useful functions that we seldom think about. In a day's time, our emotions may run the gamut from intensely positive to intensely negative and back again. You might say that they add "flavor" to our everyday experiences. Emotions are also an important component of stress, and the environmental factors that produce stress usually produce accompanying emotions.

EMOTION AND ART

From the writings of ancient civilizations to the poetry and fiction of today, emotions have long played a central role in literature. Around the world, stories about love are the most common. Shakespeare's *Romeo and Juliet* and the poetry of Elizabeth Barrett Browning are famous examples. Stories that feature strong emotions are fascinating because they reflect our own concerns and because emotions to some extent are mysterious and even paradoxical.

Emotion is also an integral component of expression in music. Opera composer Richard Wagner once described music as the language of passion. In addition to expressing the emotion of the composer, music can elicit emotion in the listener.

That is why some music makes us feel cheerful or happy and some music makes us feel sad. Philosophers as far back as Plato and Aristotle of ancient Greece believed that music could be used to calm, to bring balance, and to arouse enthusiasm. They also realized that music could be used as therapy.

Visual art is another medium through which emotion is expressed. Light and shadow, the boldness of the brush stroke, and the placement of figures and objects can impart emotional tone to a painting, for example. Artists can convey their feelings about a subject to the observer through their artwork, which in turn may produce the same emotions in the viewer.

EMOTION AND CULTURE

It was once widely thought that emotions differed from culture to culture. People from Eastern cultures, for example, seemed to show less emotion than people from Western cultures. Therefore, it was thought that emotions were learned within a culture. To test this, an anthropologist named Paul Ekman traveled to a remote area in New Guinea to study the Fore, a tribe that had not been exposed to Western civilization. Ekman carried with him photographs of Americans with facial expressions that corresponded to particular emotions. The Fore had never seen photographs of Americans before.

As Ekman told the Fore different stories, he showed them three photographs and asked them to choose the photograph with the facial expression that matched each story most closely. To his surprise, they accurately chose the corresponding photographs. Ekman also asked the Fore to make facial expressions that matched the stories. He videotaped these expressions. After he arrived back in San Francisco, he asked American research subjects to identify the emotions expressed by the Fore. The American subjects accurately identified the emotions that corresponded with the photographs of the Fore.

The results of Ekman's experiment constituted the first scientific evidence that basic emotions are universal. Although there is some disagreement among researchers about the number of basic emotions there are, most include joy, anger, fear, distress, surprise, and disgust. Each of these emotions produces a facial expression typical for that emotion (Figure 1.1). Even babies who are born blind have these same typical facial expressions for emotions.

The basic emotions also appear to be **innate**, or unlearned. They occur in a reflexlike reaction that lasts for a few seconds. It is now thought that basic emotions are automatic responses that are not under voluntary or conscious control. All cultures that have been studied so far have these basic emotions.

So why do some cultures appear to have more emotions than others? Another experiment conducted by Paul Ekman and his colleague Wallace Friesen provided a clue. They videotaped Japanese and American men as they watched film clips of events that ranged from neutral to pleasant to disgusting in content. When the subjects were shown the film clips with an interviewer present, the Japanese men showed less disgust and smiled more than the Americans. However, when the film clips were shown to the subjects in private, the facial expressions of the American and Japanese men were similar.

When the videotapes of the research subjects' expressions were shown in slow motion, an interesting discovery was made. In the research setting in which an interviewer was present, it was discovered that the Japanese men began to make the expression of disgust but masked it within fractions of a second. The researchers concluded that the two groups of subjects were operating under two different sets of "display rules" for emotions. Each culture has its own set of display rules for which types of emotional expression are considered socially acceptable. Excessive displays of emotion are

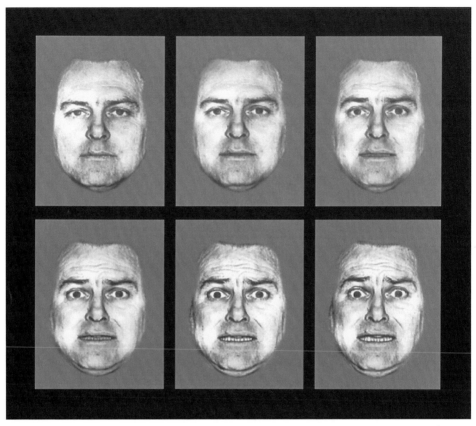

Figure 1.1 A man's face illustrates the progressive stages of fear in the series of photographs above. At top left is a face showing a neutral expression, while the face at the bottom right shows the greatest amount of fear. The expression of a number of emotions, including fear, is innate and universal to all cultures.

considered rude in the Japanese culture, so emotional expression is more suppressed.

Another group of emotions is known as **higher cognitive emotions**. Most scientists include love, jealousy, pride, shame, guilt, embarrassment, and envy in this group. Unlike basic emotions, which may occur in milliseconds, higher cognitive emotions usually develop over a period of days, weeks, or longer. Higher cognitive emotions, as their name implies, are also more influenced by conscious thought. (Cognitive processes in the brain enable us to be aware, to think, to know, to learn, and to make judgments.) There are no specific facial expressions associated with these emotions, and they vary more from culture to culture. Like basic emotions, though, they are universal and are found in every culture that has been studied.

EMOTION AND REASON

Since the time of Plato, emotions have been viewed by many Western philosophers as obstacles to reason and intelligent thinking. The idea that the opposite may be true—that emotions may be vital to reason—has only recently become popular. Research in psychology and **neuroscience** (the study of the brain and nervous system) now appears to support this view. A combination of reason and emotion seems to be important to intelligent action.

For example, fear enables us to respond appropriately to danger, whereas anger prepares us to fight when necessary. The surprise reaction enables us to stop and focus on novel stimuli so that we can respond to them appropriately. Disgust causes us to avoid things that may be poisonous or infectious. For example, the sight and odor of spoiled food causes us to experience the emotion of disgust.

WHAT IS STRESS?

A stressful situation is often accompanied by negative emotions such as fear, anger, or embarrassment. Stress is sometimes defined as a "perceived threat" that is caused by environmental factors. In other words, for an event to be stressful, the brain must first perceive that the event poses some type of threat. These environmental factors, known as **stressors**, may be physical in nature, such as the presence of a ferocious wild animal bounding toward you or the sight of rising floodwaters after a storm. They may also be psychological in nature, such as an argument with one's best friend or an impending final exam.

Prior to the 1940s, *stress* as a scientific term was primarily used by engineers to describe the forces exerted on a building

Neurasthenia

Neurasthenia was a diagnostic term used by physicians during the last three decades of the nineteenth century for patients who could not meet the demands of their roles in life. This term, which has not been used in the United States since the 1920s, was proposed in 1869 by American neurologist George Miller Beard, who believed that the fast pace of modern industrial life could lead to a "circuit overload" and produce a weakness in the nervous system. This new malady was thought by physicians of the time to be found primarily in middle- and upper-class women and was believed to constitute a national epidemic. During the national obsession with this disorder during the late nineteenth century, paintings of women diagnosed with neurasthenia portrayed them as pale, listless, and introspective. Known also as "nervous exhaustion" and characterized by symptoms such as irrational fears, excessive anxiety, and unexplainable fatigue, this label performed a social function by giving patients what appeared to be a scientifically valid explanation for their inability to function. Cardiologist Richard Fogoros believes that these patients were suffering from dysautonomia, an imbalance of the autonomic nervous system. According to him, some of the diagnoses that would be given to them today are chronic fatigue syndrome, fibromyalgia, anxiety, panic attacks, and irritable bowel syndrome.

or other structure. Since that time, it has been the subject of much scientific investigation and debate. Over the centuries, it was recognized that causes of illness could be nonphysical and that the hurried pace of life could be responsible for illness. "Nervous exhaustion" was an accepted diagnosis by the nineteenth century.

In the twentieth century, the acceptance of stress as a disturbance of **homeostasis**, or balance, was at the center of intense scientific research. This continuing research has focused on understanding stress and its effects on the body and mind. It has also focused on finding ways to reduce stress or to minimize its effects. This has become increasingly important as the pace of modern life has continued to hasten steadily.

In the twenty-first century, we have come to accept stress as an uncomfortable but seemingly necessary part of our daily lives. How well we cope with stress determines many things, such as our ability to reach our goals and maintain our health under the pressures of modern life. By understanding stress and how it can affect us, we can begin to take steps to harness its energy but at the same time avoid its negative impact.

In the following chapters, we will look first at emotion and then at stress. Emotions and stress result from a complex interplay of the body's nervous, immune, and endocrine systems. We will learn how emotions are regulated, how they interact with our thinking skills, and how they can affect our health. Then we will learn about the components of the stress response, environmental factors that can cause stress, the effects of stress on our health, and how we can cope with stress.

■ **Learn more about the contents of this chapter**   Search the Internet for *stressor*, *homeostasis*, and *neuroscience*.

2 Experience and Expression of Emotion

As Jane slid into her seat moments before the bell rang, the stack of papers on the teacher's desk caught her eye. That term paper she had put so much effort into should be in that stack! The teacher rose from her chair and looked over at Jane as she picked the papers up from her desk. Holding her breath, Jane looked for some type of expression—a smile, a frown, or even a sparkle in the teacher's eye. But there was none. Jane's heart pounded and her hopes rose and sank as the teacher made her way around the classroom and finally handed Jane the last paper in the stack.

Hardly daring to look, Jane finally risked a peek and saw penned neatly across the top of the page, "Excellent paper! You should consider a writing career!" Jane's worried look was quickly replaced with a smile. She looked up to see the teacher watching her with the hint of a smile at the corners of her mouth. Noticing the glum look on her best friend's face in the seat next to her, Jane suppressed her smile and went about getting her pen and notebook out to take notes for class. Inwardly she rejoiced, for this had been the most interesting yet challenging assignment of the school year.

Scientists distinguish between the experience of emotion and the expression of emotion. The emotional experience is an internal, private affair that only the person having it knows about. Emotional expression is the way in which we communicate our emotional experiences to others. The expression of emotion not only allows others to know what we are feeling but also allows them to predict the behaviors that may accompany particular emotions.

COMPONENTS OF EMOTION

The brain and the body work together to produce the emotional experience. Components of the emotional experience include a **physiological** response, feelings, and cognitive activities. Emotional behavior is a component of emotional expression, which we will discuss later in this chapter. The neural, or nervous, system and activities that underlie the other components and that can be considered an additional component of emotion will be discussed later.

Probably the most familiar component of an emotional experience is the feeling component, the sensation of an emotion, which uniquely identifies that emotion. For example, the feeling of sadness as we say good-bye to old friends is very different from the feeling of happiness we experience when we see them again after a long absence.

Cognitive activities, such as thoughts and mental images, are also part of an emotion. These activities may not only be part of an emotion but also may actually trigger an emotion. Daydreaming is a good example. Most daydreams consist of vivid imagery accompanied by a variety of emotions.

There are physiological, or bodily, changes that vary somewhat with different emotions. The heart may speed up or slow down. Changes in the rate of breathing and in the temperature of the skin may occur. Muscle tension may increase or decrease. These changes are triggered by an interaction between the nervous system and the endocrine system, which we will discuss in more detail later.

Neural processes, or the activity of neurons, form another component that is responsible for triggering or generating the physiological, cognitive, and feeling components of emotion. Neurons are the cells from which brain structures are made. Directly or indirectly, they send neural signals to other brain cells and to all parts of the body.

EXPRESSION OF EMOTION

We communicate our emotions to others through behaviors. Our emotional behaviors also provide information to people about our intentions to act on our emotions. Emotions are communicated through facial expressions, tone of voice, vocalizations, touch, interpersonal distance, postural changes, gestures, gait (the way we walk), and other physical movements, Nonverbal communication of emotions is also known as **body language.** In addition to facial expression, many of our emotional behaviors are universal in that they are similar in different cultures.

FACIAL EXPRESSIONS

The primary nonverbal way in which people communicate emotions is through facial expressions. Paul Ekman and others have studied the muscles of the face and have identified the 43 facial muscles that participate in the expression of particular emotions (Figure 2.1). Ekman and Friesen developed the Facial Action Coding System in the 1970s to describe how each facial muscle contracts, either alone or in combination with other facial muscles, during different emotional expressions. Different parts of the same muscle can also participate in the expression of different emotions.

One research finding is that spontaneous expression of a particular emotion and posed expression of the same emotion involve slightly different muscle groups. For example, a spontaneous smile involves contracting the orbicularis oculi muscle

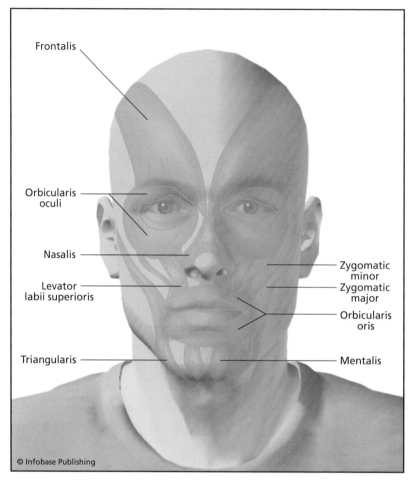

Frontalis

Orbicularis
oculi

Nasalis

Levator
labii superioris

Triangularis

Zygomatic
minor

Zygomatic
major

Orbicularis
oris

Mentalis

© Infobase Publishing

Figure 2.1 From top to bottom: The frontalis muscle raises the eyebrows and causes the forehead to wrinkle up. When contracted, the orbicularis oculi muscle narrows the eye opening and constricts the skin at the corner of the eye. One part of the nasalis muscle constricts the nostrils, and another part flares the nostrils. The lateral part of the levator labii superioris raises the entire lip, and the inner part also wrinkles the nose. Both the zygomatic major and the zygomatic minor muscles lift the corners of the mouth. Forming most of the lip tissue, the orbicularis oris muscle controls the shape and size of the mouth and is important in speech and emotional expression. The triangularis muscle pulls the corners of the mouth down, as in a frown. Thought to be associated with concentration or with doubt, the mentalis muscle pushes the chin upward so that the chin wrinkles and the lower lip curves upward to produce an inverted *U*.

(which encircles the eye) as well as the zygomaticus major muscle (which runs diagonally from the mouth to the eye and lifts the cheek and the corner of the mouth). The orbicularis oculi muscle does not contract during a posed smile. You can tell a posed smile from a genuine smile by the absence of the little crinkles around the eyes. Duchenne Guillaume, a French neurologist, first described this difference in 1862. As a result, the genuine smile is now known as the **Duchenne smile**.

FACIAL FEEDBACK HYPOTHESIS

Paul Ekman and his colleagues came up with the hypothesis that if you contract the appropriate facial muscles for a particular emotion, you will experience that emotion to some degree. To test this hypothesis, they performed an experiment in which they gave research subjects step-by-step instructions for contracting facial muscles appropriate for the six basic emotions. The subjects were only told what movements to make. They were not told that they were simulating facial expressions for an emotion.

As the subjects responded, Ekman's team measured physiological responses and found that they changed, much as they did with genuine emotions. Heart rate, for example, increased with fear or anger expressions. Skin temperature increased with angry expressions and decreased with fear expressions. Heart rate decreased with happy expressions, with skin temperature remaining unchanged. It is not clear yet whether the autonomic responses under these circumstances are innate or whether these are conditioned, or learned, responses.

VOCAL CHANGES IN EMOTION

Vocalizations are an important source of information about emotions. Changes in loudness, pitch, tempo, fluency, and inflection all serve to signal emotional states. **Vocal cues** are expressed in patterns that are typical of the different emotions.

Theories of Emotion

Scientists have debated for more than a century which occurs first: the bodily changes or the brain's perception of an emotion. William James, a nineteenth-century American psychologist, thought that an external stimulus (e.g., the sight of a dangerous animal) caused the brain to trigger physiological responses, which then were perceived and interpreted by the brain as an emotion. James borrowed some of his ideas from the Danish psychologist Carl Lange, so the theory is known as the James-Lange theory.

Physiologist Walter Cannon disagreed with the James-Lange theory. Since physiological changes are shared by more than one emotion, Cannon believed that nerve impulses go simultaneously to the cerebral cortex (the thinking brain) and the thalamus, the brain area responsible for triggering the physiological responses. He thought that emotions and the physiological changes that accompany them were parallel

James-Lange Theory

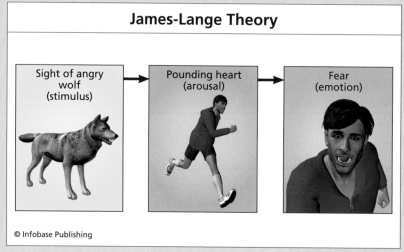

Sight of angry wolf (stimulus) → Pounding heart (arousal) → Fear (emotion)

© Infobase Publishing

The James-Lange theory of emotion.

Cannon-Bard Theory

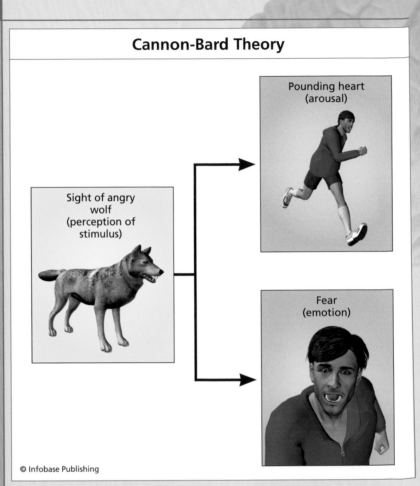

Pounding heart (arousal)

Sight of angry wolf (perception of stimulus)

Fear (emotion)

© Infobase Publishing

The Cannon-Bard theory of emotion.

processes produced independently of each other. Philip Bard modified Cannon's original theory somewhat, so the theory is known today as the Cannon-Bard theory of emotion. Subsequent research has shown that the process of experiencing emotion is much more complex than either of these earlier theories, but some elements of each theory are still held to be true.

For example, vocal cues associated with happiness include a fast tempo, moderate loudness variation, and an extreme pitch variation. Vocal cues for sadness are characterized by a decrease in intensity, pitch, and tempo. Humans tend to be very accurate in their assessment of emotional states from vocal cues. People are capable of making fine discriminations among these complex stimuli.

BODILY MOVEMENTS

Posture, gestures, and gait also communicate emotion. People identify emotions from these nonverbal cues at levels that are better than chance. There is also a lot of similarity across

The Polygraph Test

The polygraph, or "lie detector" machine, is in reality an emotion detector. It actually detects physiological responses to emotion, such as perspiration, changes in heart rate, or changes in breathing rate. The subject is asked two types of questions: control questions and critical questions. Control questions make the subject a little nervous and elicit a small response. Critical questions are related to the issue at hand, such as a crime that has been committed. A truthful answer should elicit a smaller response than the control questions. Theoretically, a dishonest answer will be accompanied by a physiological response that is larger than that for the control questions.

Psychologists such as Leonard Saxe and David Lykken have questioned the validity of these tests. They contend that the polygraph is more of a fear detector than a lie detector. If a critical question were to upset an innocent person, a false positive would be registered. Fear and anxiety produce the same physiological response as guilt. This elicits erroneous results

cultures in the movements that are used to express various emotions. The degree of erectness of posture, for example, can communicate anything from sadness (slumped posture) to anger and aggression (erect posture).

Movements of the limbs and gait also communicate emotions. Swaggering movements can communicate pride or anger. Running away from something may communicate fear. Reduced arm swing usually accompanies sadness. Repeated and rhythmic upward movements of the arms can express joy. A heavy-footed gait can communicate anger. Longer strides may reveal pride. A faster pace indicates happiness, whereas a slower gait can communicate sadness.

in about one-third of these tests. The polygraph test can also be outsmarted by methods such as biting one's tongue during control questions to increase the physiological response. This would result in a smaller difference in response between control questions and critical questions and thus would provide a false negative result.

There is such a high error rate with the standard polygraph that Congress in 1988 prohibited its use for most nongovernmental testing. A variation of this procedure, called the guilty knowledge test, is considered to be more scientifically valid and has become useful in criminal investigations. A person guilty of a crime should have stronger physiological responses when details about the crime scene are mentioned. If a suspect reacts to a number of specific details that only someone familiar with the crime would know, it is reasonable to suspect that he may be guilty of the crime or was present when the crime was committed.

A multitude of gestures, some of them subtle, some of them expansive, communicate emotions. Anxiety may be expressed by wringing one's hands or fidgeting with one's hair. Anger may be communicated through threat gestures. Fear is often signaled by the hands shielding the face.

TOUCH

Touch is one of the ways in which we communicate emotion, particularly to people with whom we are close emotionally. On the positive side, it can range from the gentle touch of a mother's hand, to the warm embrace of friends, to the passionate kiss of newlyweds. On the negative side, it can range from a warning touch on the arm to a kick in the shins or a punch in the face.

There are individual, gender, and cultural differences in the expression of emotion through touch. Some individuals are more comfortable with expressing emotion through touch than others. In general, females tend to communicate emotions through touch more than do males. Some cultures use touch to communicate emotions more than others.

INTERPERSONAL SPACE

Our **interpersonal space** is the amount of space that we maintain between ourselves and other individuals. This space is smaller for friends and family than it is for casual acquaintances or strangers. Intruding into this space can communicate anger or aggression. Reduction of this space for family and friends can indicate affection. Increasing one's usual interpersonal space can signal dislike or fear.

The average interpersonal space differs across cultures. Studies have shown that Americans and people in northern European countries such as England and France require more interpersonal space than other cultures.

GENDER DIFFERENCES IN EMOTION

When responding to questionnaires, women report a greater intensity of emotions, both positive and negative, than men do. Except possibly for anger, women are also more facially expressive of emotions than men. Measurement of the activity of facial muscles shows that emotion-appropriate responses of facial muscles to pictures of happy or angry faces are greater in women than in men. Crying behavior is found more frequently in women, whereas men are more physically aggressive than women. Women also smile more than men during social interactions. Except for reading cues for anger, at which men are superior, women are more adept at decoding nonverbal cues for emotions. Some of these gender differences may be biological, and others may be a result of socialization by parents and peers.

■ **Learn more about the contents of this chapter**   Search the Internet for *body language*, *facial feedback hypothesis*, and *interpersonal space*.

3 | Neuroscience Basics

Jonathan watched the luminous red sun sink to meet the ocean and then slip beneath the horizon, leaving streaks of orange and red across the sky in all directions. The relaxing sound of the waves at the foot of the cliff below was music to his ears as he set about making a campfire for the evening. The aroma of the cooking food filled his nostrils as he prepared to make camp for the night. His day had consisted of walking barefoot on the beach and swimming in the sparkling waters. The sand had been warm and coarse beneath his feet, and the coolness of the ocean had been exhilarating. Seagulls and ocean birds had been his only companions as he enjoyed the serenity of the seashore. Tomorrow he would head back to the city, with its hustle and bustle, the incessant blaring of horns, and chatter of people's voices.

All the sights and sounds and other sensations that made Jonathan's day so enjoyable were made available to him by the intricate workings of the nervous system. Physical and chemical stimuli were received through Jonathan's sense organs and transmitted by nerves to his brain. The brain interprets the signals from the sense organs and then reacts to them. If action is needed, the brain sends out nerve impulses that tell the body how to respond. Therefore, the brain can be considered the central command post of the body. The nerves function as fiber highways, carrying information to and from the brain.

NEURONAL STRUCTURE

Like other cells, neurons have a cell body that is covered with a cell membrane and contains tiny structures called **organelles**. These organelles include the nucleus and other structures that carry out the activities of the cell. (The cell body of a neuron is called a **soma**.) Unlike other cells, neurons have long extensions called **axons** that carry a signal *to* other neurons. Neurons also have a number of shorter extensions called **dendrites** that receive messages *from* other neurons (Figure 3.1). Some neurons have dendrites that are so branched that they are referred to as a **dendritic tree**. On the dendrites are tiny thornlike protuberances called **dendritic spines**.

THE NEURAL SIGNAL

Neurons are unique in that they transmit information through an electrochemical signal. Electrical signals carry information down the length of the nerve fibers. When the electrical signal, called an **action potential**, arrives at the end, or terminal, of an axon, it causes neurochemicals called **neurotransmitters** to be released from the **axon terminal** (Figure 3.2). Neurotransmitters diffuse across the **synapse** (tiny gap) between the nerve ending of one neuron and the cell body of the next neuron and carry the neural signal to the receiving neuron.

NEUROTRANSMITTERS

There are four basic groups of neurotransmitters: acetylcholine, amino acids, monoamines, and peptides. In the 1920s, German physiologist Otto Loewi discovered acetylcholine, making it the first neurotransmitter discovered. The monoamines include

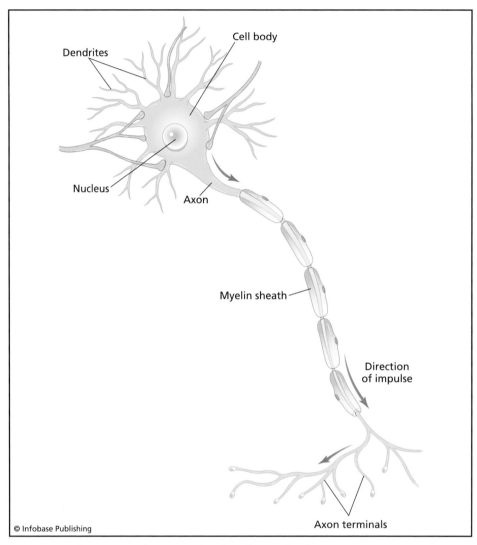

Dendrites

Cell body

Nucleus

Axon

Myelin sheath

Direction
of impulse

Axon terminals

© Infobase Publishing

Figure 3.1 The neuron is the basic signaling unit of the nervous system. Neural signals from thousands of other neurons are received by the dendrites and summed together. If the combined signal is sufficient, it causes the neuron to fire its own neural signal, which travels down the axon to the axon terminals. The axon terminals connect to numerous other neurons, to which they transmit the signal by the release of neurotransmitters. The myelin sheath that surrounds the axon of some neurons provides insulation that enables the action potential to travel faster.

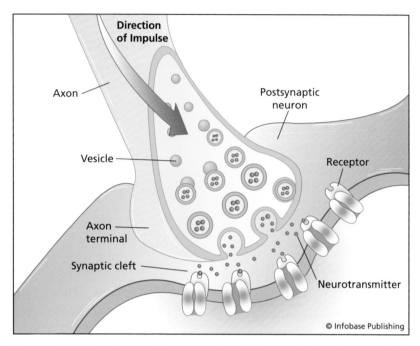

Direction of Impulse

Axon

Vesicle

Axon terminal

Synaptic cleft

Postsynaptic neuron

Receptor

Neurotransmitter

© Infobase Publishing

Figure 3.2 Neurotransmitters are stored in small structures called vesicles in the axon terminals of neurons. When the action potential reaches the axon terminal, neurotransmitter molecules are released into the synaptic cleft. Neurotransmitter receptors are proteins in the postsynaptic membrane to which neurotransmitter molecules attach, causing changes in the electrical qualities of the postsynaptic cell membrane that may contribute to the firing of an action potential by the postsynaptic neuron.

norepinephrine, epinephrine, dopamine, and serotonin. Glutamate and aspartate are the most abundant excitatory amino acid neurotransmitters. Gamma-aminobutyric acid (GABA) and glycine are the most abundant inhibitory amino acid neurotransmitters. The combined effects of neurotransmitters released from all the nerve endings that synapse on a particular neuron determine whether that neuron will transmit an action potential down its axon. For the neuron to fire an action potential, the effects of excitatory neurotransmitters must exceed those of the inhibitory neurotransmitters.

Neurotransmitters produce their actions by attaching to special proteins called **receptors**, into which they fit as a key does in a lock. **Neurotransmitter receptors** are usually found embedded in the cell membrane at the synapse. Many drugs, including herbal remedies used before neurotransmitters were ever discovered, attach to these receptors. These drugs act by either mimicking the actions of the neurotransmitters or blocking their action. Those that mimic the actions of neurotransmitters are called **agonists**. Those that block the action of neurotransmitters are called **antagonists**.

DIVISIONS OF THE NERVOUS SYSTEM

There are two major divisions of the nervous system: the **central nervous system** and the **peripheral nervous system**. The central nervous system is comprised of the brain and the spinal cord, both of which are enclosed in the protective bony encasements of the skull and spinal column. The spinal cord carries messages from the body to the brain and from the brain to the body.

The peripheral nervous system consists of all nervous system components outside (peripheral to) the central nervous system. There are two major subdivisions of the peripheral nervous system: the **somatic nervous system** and the **autonomic nervous system**. The somatic nervous system carries sensory information from the sense organs to the central nervous system and carries motor commands from the central nervous system that control voluntary and reflexive muscle movement. The autonomic nervous system is the peripheral nervous system division that controls the contraction of involuntary muscles in the blood vessels, internal organs, and glands.

There are three divisions of the autonomic nervous system. The **sympathetic nervous system** is the division of the autonomic nervous system that prepares the body for fight or flight in a threatening situation. The **parasympathetic nervous system** is the autonomic nervous system division that maintains normal function in the body and returns the body to normal function after sympathetic activation. Within the walls and underneath the lining of the gastrointestinal tract are networks (**plexi**) of neurons that operate independently of the rest of the nervous system. This third division of the autonomic nervous system, the enteric nervous system, has sometimes been called "the second brain" as a result.

ORGANIZATION OF THE BRAIN

Seen from the outside, the brain consists of two large, convoluted **cerebral hemispheres** sitting atop the much smaller brain stem, which continues below as the spinal cord. Perched atop the back of the brain stem just below the cerebral hemispheres is the **cerebellum**. Moving upward from the spinal cord, the divisions of the **brain stem** are the medulla, the pons, and the midbrain. Above the midbrain and concealed by the folds of the cerebral hemispheres is the **diencephalon**. Here are found the thalamus and the hypothalamus, two structures that are very important in the emotional experience.

If the brain is sliced straight down between the cerebral hemispheres, a **midsagittal** section is produced that exposes the midline structures inside the brain (Figure 3.3). Creating a midsagittal section allows us to see that most of the structures of the brain occur in pairs, with one structure of each pair on either side of the midline. The most obvious of these is the pair of cerebral hemispheres.

CEREBRAL HEMISPHERES

The structures on either side of the brain communicate with each other through bundles of nerve fibers called **commissures**. The largest of these commissures is called the **corpus callosum**. Beneath the corpus callosum is a double-layered membrane

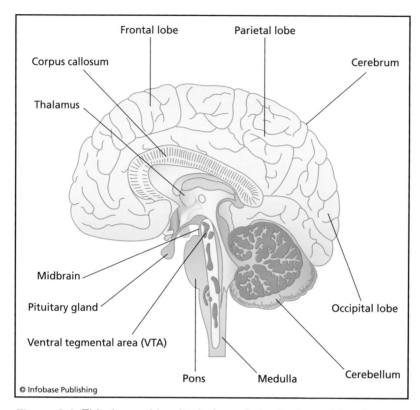

Figure 3.3 This is a midsagittal view of the brain and is what you would see if the brain were cut down the middle between the two cerebral hemispheres. Most brain structures are paired: There is one on each side of the brain.

called the **septum pellucidum**, which separates two fluid-filled **lateral ventricles**. The fluid in the lateral ventricles empties into the third ventricle and then into the fourth ventricle, from which it flows out and around the brain. This fluid, called the **cerebrospinal fluid**, acts as a cushion for the brain within the skull. Other functions of the cerebrospinal fluid include carrying nutrients to—and waste products away from—the brain. The cerebrospinal fluid is produced by special clusters of cells in the lining of the **cerebral ventricles** known as the choroids plexi.

The lateral ventricles are found inside the cerebral hemispheres. The paired thalami and hypothalami form the walls and floor of the third ventricle. The cerebellum, a structure important in the coordination of movement, forms the roof of the fourth ventricle, and the brain stem forms its floor.

The **cerebral cortex** consists of a thin layer of nervous tissue folded like a crumpled piece of paper. This shape allows a much larger surface area to fit within the confines of the skull. About two-thirds of this outer layer of the cerebral hemispheres is found within its folds. Underneath the cerebral cortex, which consists of six layers of neurons, or nerve cells, are found the fiber tracts that carry the signals from the nerve cells to other brain structures and downward toward the spinal cord.

LOBES OF THE CEREBRAL CORTEX

There are four large lobes, or divisions, of the cerebral cortex (Figure 3.4). The **frontal lobe** is in front of the **central sulcus**, which is a deep fissure extending horizontally across the cerebral hemispheres. The deep groove between the hemispheres is called the **central fissure**. (A **sulcus** lies between folds, or **gyri**, of the brain and is not quite as deep as a **fissure**.) Surrounding the back "pole" of the brain is the **occipital lobe**. The **temporal lobe** is found in front of the occipital lobe and extends downward from the large groove called the **lateral fissure**. The **parietal lobe** is found above the lateral fissure between the occipital lobe and the frontal lobe.

SENSORY CORTEX

Except for the sense of smell, all sensory stimuli travel first to the thalamus in the diencephalon for processing before being sent to areas of the cerebral cortex that are specific for each sense. These areas are known as **primary sensory cortices** and are the first place in the cerebral cortex where information from the sense organs is processed after it is relayed through

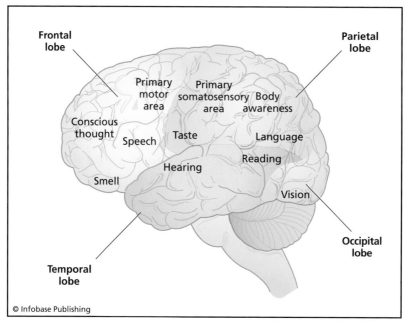

Figure 3.4 Each of the four lobes of the cerebral hemisphere specializes in particular functions. Sensory input from the eyes is received
and interpreted by the occipital lobe. Auditory input is received and
interpreted by the temporal lobe, which also is involved in feeling emotion, understanding speech, and forming memories. Somatosensory
information is received and interpreted by the parietal lobe, which
also integrates somatosensory information with information from the
other senses. The frontal lobe is in charge of thinking, speech, the
control of emotions, and the planning and control of movements.

the thalamus. For example, visual stimuli are sent to the occipital lobe, and the sense of touch and other body senses are sent
to the parietal lobe. Auditory (hearing) stimuli go first to the
temporal lobe inside the lateral sulcus. Taste stimuli are sent to
an area of cortex called the **insula**, which is hidden underneath
the **opercula**, or outer edges, of the frontal, parietal, and temporal lobes where they come together. Unlike stimuli from the
other senses, olfactory (smell) stimuli go to olfactory primary
sensory cortex before going to the thalamus.

After being processed in the primary sensory cortices, sensory information is relayed to the appropriate secondary sensory cortices. (Olfactory stimuli are relayed from the thalamus to the olfactory secondary cortex.) From the secondary sensory cortex, processed information may be sent to tertiary or **polymodal cortex**. (Polymodal cortex is where information from one or more senses is integrated.) All levels of cortex higher than primary are known as **association cortices**. The end result of this complex integration and interpretation of sensory data is our perception of our internal and external environments.

SUBCORTICAL NUCLEI

Deep within the cerebral hemispheres are found paired **nuclei**, or groups of neurons that perform certain similar functions. On either side of the lateral ventricles lie a paired group of nuclei that are important in movement. These are called the **basal ganglia**, and they include the caudate nucleus, the globus pallidus, the putamen, and the subthalamic nucleus. A nucleus in the midbrain, the substantia nigra, is also considered to be a functional part of this group. A little farther laterally and ventrally (downward) are found the paired hippocampi, which are elongated C-shaped structures that are important in emotion, learning, and memory. Just in front of the base of each hippocampus is an almond-shaped structure called the **amygdala**, which also performs important functions in the emotional process.

LIMBIC SYSTEM

The amygdala and hippocampus, as well as certain nuclei of the hypothalamus and the thalamus, are part of the **limbic system** (Figure 3.5). They communicate with each other by nerve fiber pathways. Certain areas of the cerebral cortex are also considered part of the limbic system. These include the **cingulate gyrus,** which can be seen in the midsagittal section as the area

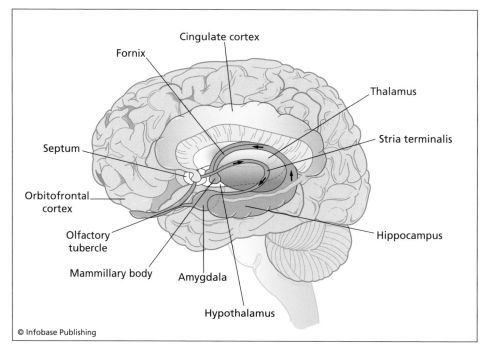

Figure 3.5 Shown in this drawing are both cortical and subcortical structures of the limbic system. The stria terminalis is a major fiber highway that carries inputs and outputs of the amygdala. The fornix is a major fiber highway of the hippocampus. Physiologist Paul MacLean gave the limbic system its name because it forms a limbus, or ring, around the thalamus.

of cerebral cortex arching over the corpus callosum. Some scientists include the **septal nuclei** that lie just below the septum pellucidum in the front of the brain. The **nucleus accumbens**, which is often called the "pleasure center" because of its role in reward, is sometimes included also.

Areas of the cortex that are found on the ventral, or underside, of the front of the brain are considered part of the limbic system. These include the **orbitofrontal cortex**, which lies directly above the bony orbits that contain the eyes. Also included is the **ventral medial prefrontal cortex**, which lies on either side of the midline between the two orbitofrontal cortices. At the front of the brain, just before the brain folds under, is found the **dorsal prefrontal cortex**, which is also included in the limbic system.

RESEARCH METHODS OF NEUROSCIENTISTS

Neuroscientists use a variety of research techniques to study the nervous system and its functions. These range from those that allow scientists to study the nervous system at a molecular or cellular level to those that allow them to study the behaviors controlled by the nervous system. Let's take a look at some of the more commonly used techniques that we will encounter in the chapters ahead.

Lesion Techniques

Much of the knowledge we have of brain functions comes from **lesion studies** in animals. With the lesion technique, a particular area of the animal's brain is destroyed experimentally. The animal's behavior and physiological functions are then observed to determine whether there are any changes. Since multiple areas of the brain are usually involved in any given function, the process of determining the precise contribution of each of these areas to a particular function can be rather complicated. It may involve lesions of individual structures as well as lesions of various combinations of structures and the nerve pathways that connect them.

For obvious reasons, lesion studies in humans are restricted to preexisting lesions that have occurred as the result of trauma, disease, or surgery. Subjects with brain lesions are compared on various tests with patients who have no detectable brain lesions. Significant differences between the two groups in a particular function may indicate that it is the normal function of the brain area that was damaged. Many times the areas damaged are later confirmed by autopsy, and the tissues are studied at a microscopic level. Much of the earlier knowledge of human brain function was obtained in this manner. In fact, that was the only method available to relate structure and function in the human brain before the development of modern **neuroimaging techniques**.

Neuroimaging Techniques

Neuroimaging techniques make it possible to observe the brain in a noninvasive manner. Activity in various brain areas can be observed during different behavioral tasks or during exposure to various stimuli. Several neuroimaging techniques have become available in recent years. Two techniques that have become particularly useful in studying structure/function relationships are the PET scan and the fMRI technique.

The **positron emission tomography (PET) scan** is often used to measure metabolic rate in brain areas, particularly while observing behaviors to which these areas may be related. A very small dose of a **radioactive tracer** such as radiolabeled **2-deoxyglucose (2-DG)** is injected to begin the experiment. After being injected into an animal, this **analog** (structurally similar compound) of glucose is taken up by the cell just as glucose is. Since 2-DG cannot be metabolized by the cell, it remains in the cell until it is eventually degraded. The more active a cell is, the more glucose it takes up for its energy requirements. Consequently, cells that are more active take up more 2-DG and therefore contain more radioactivity.

The scanner into which the subject's head is placed detects the positrons emitted from radioactive atoms attached to the 2-DG as they decay. (A positron is a positively charged particle that has the same mass that an electron does.) After analyzing the data, a computer program generates a picture that resembles a brain slice, with the more-active areas "lit up" with color that changes with the intensity of the radioactivity, such as red for the most active areas, yellow for the next-most-active areas, and so on.

PET scans are also used to measure the concentration of neurochemicals of interest in the human brain. A precursor from which the body normally makes a particular neurotransmitter substance (for example) is attached to a radioactive tracer and injected into the bloodstream. This radiolabeled compound is taken up and utilized by neurons that synthesize the neurotransmitter, resulting in a buildup of radioactivity in those neurons. An hour after injection of the tracer, a PET scan is done, and the areas of the brain that utilized the neurotransmitter precursor can be visualized and the amount of radioactivity measured.

Magnetic resonance imaging (MRI) is a neuroimaging technique that generates images of horizontal, saggital (longitudinal), or coronal (parallel to the face) sections of the brain. Hydrogen atoms consist of one proton, and two of them are contained in each water molecule in the body. While the subject is lying inside the tube, or bore, of the MRI machine, a powerful magnetic current is passed through the bore parallel to the orientation of the subject's body. This magnetic field causes most of the hydrogen atoms to line up toward either the head or the feet. Pulses of radio waves specific to hydrogen are then directed toward the brain. When the radio frequency pulses stop, the hydrogen atoms return to their previous alignment and release excess energy, which creates a signal that is detected by the MRI machine and transmitted to a computer for analysis.

Functional magnetic resonance imaging (fMRI) is an adaptation of MRI technology that allows scientists to detect the areas of the brain that are activated during a particular activity. Since the magnetic properties of blood are affected by its oxygen content, MRI can be used to detect changes in blood oxygenation levels of brain areas involved in an activity. (Active areas of the brain have increases in oxygen levels,

Neurogenesis

Until the early 1990s, scientific dogma held that neurogenesis, or the birth of new neurons, did not occur in the adult brain. (This belief prevailed despite published reports of neurogenesis in various animals.) Puzzled by evidence of neurogenesis she found while studying the death of neurons induced by stress hormones, Elizabeth Gould convinced the scientific community that neurogenesis was indeed real—at least in rats. Later she reported neurogenesis in marmosets (1998) and in macaque monkeys (1999).

In 1998, Peter Eriksson of Sweden, Fred Gage of the Salk Institute, and their colleagues reported the results of a project in which they injected a radiolabeled analog of thymidine, a nucleotide, in terminally ill patients. (Nucleotides are building blocks for DNA.) Postmortem examination of the brains of these patients demonstrated that the nucleotides had become part of the DNA of new cells in the dentate gyrus of the hippocampus. This was the first proof that neurogenesis takes place in adult human brains.

The subgranular layer of the dentate gyrus of the hippocampus is one of two areas in the adult brain where neurogenesis occurs on a regular basis. Newly formed neurons from the subgranular layer migrate to the overlying granule cell layer and become functional neurons. Nearby is the subependymal layer, which lies just underneath the ependymal layer that lines the lateral ventricles. New cells from this layer migrate to the olfactory bulb, where they become interneurons that connect other olfactory neurons.

Voluntary exercise and learning have been shown to increase the rate of neurogenesis. In 2005, Robert Sapolsky's research team reported that rats that were kept awake during half of their rest phase on training days had impaired learning of a water maze task. Even more significant, the increase in neurogenesis

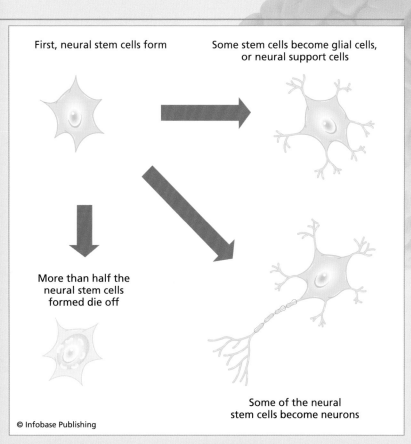

First, neural stem cells form

Some stem cells become glial cells, or neural support cells

More than half the neural stem cells formed die off

Some of the neural stem cells become neurons

© Infobase Publishing

New neurons and glial cells are produced from neural stem cells in the dentate gyrus and the subventricular zone (SVZ), areas of the brain where neurogenesis continues throughout adulthood. Most new neurons formed in these brain areas fail to make functional dendritic connections and subsequently die. Those that survive are capable of sending and receiving neural signals just like the neurons surrounding them that have been present since birth.

that usually accompanies learning in this task was abolished by the restriction of sleep. Chronic stress decreases the rate of neurogenesis. Neurogenesis is also decreased in the brains of severely depressed people. Stimulating neurogenesis is now thought to have potential for relieving depression and repairing damaged brains.

glucose consumption, and blood flow.) This information can be superimposed over a standard MRI to produce a "map" of brain function.

Electrophysiological Techniques

Electrical activity of individual neurons in animals can be recorded by inserting a **microelectrode** into the brain and lowering it to the appropriate level. Microelectrodes may be used for **acute**, or short-term, observation of neural activity while an animal is anesthetized. Or they may be attached to tiny electrical sockets that are cemented to the animal's skull for **chronic**, or long-term, studies of neural activity. Electrical activity is recorded while the animal is sleeping or engaging in various behaviors. After being amplified, the electrical signals transmitted from microelectodes are displayed on the screen of an **oscilloscope** and can be stored in a computer for future study.

Macroelectrodes are used to study neural activity of all the neurons, potentially thousands to millions in number, in a particular brain area. Unsharpened wires lowered into the brain are used in animal studies. In human studies, metal disks to which an electrical-conducting paste is applied are attached to the scalp at predetermined locations. Neural activity transmitted from macroelectrodes is amplified and then recorded on a paper strip that moves past the tips of a series of tiny pens that move up and down relative to the electrical signal that reaches them. The result is an **electroencephalogram (EEG)**, a series of wavelike forms that describe the activity of an area of the brain over time. Newer technology makes a computer display possible instead. Changes in these wave forms can be seen during the different stages of sleep and during different activities during waking.

These are but a few of the many and varied techniques used by neuroscientists to study the brain and nervous system. Quite often, neuroscientists will use a combination of techniques in their studies, which allows them to ask the same question in a variety of different ways. The results can be combined to give a broader, more integrated answer than could have been obtained with just one technique.

■ **Learn more about the contents of this chapter** Search the Internet for *neuroimaging, electrophysiology*, and *neurogenesis*.

4 | The Biology of Emotion

An emotion begins with the detection of a **stimulus**. This stimulus may come from either our internal or external physical environment, or it may be part of a memory of an emotion-causing event. It may even be a product of our imagination as we engage in daydreaming. Regardless of its source, this stimulus sets in motion processes in the brain and body that we interpret as emotion.

A number of brain structures are important in the control of the different components of the emotional response (Figure 4.1). Although the emotional process involves the interaction of many different areas, there are a few key players. For example, the amygdala is responsible for triggering the emotional response by sending messages to the hypothalamus and other areas of the brain. The hypothalamus in turn triggers the physiological arousal inherent in emotion. Whereas the amygdala specializes (although not exclusively) in negative emotions, the nucleus accumbens is important in the experience of positive emotions and is a key structure in the reward system. Behavioral activation, in the form of aggressive or defensive movements, is triggered by the periaqueductal gray. The prefrontal cortex is important in integrating emotions with cognitive functions and in keeping emotional arousal under control.

AMYGDALA

Sensory information travels to the appropriate sensory cortices to be processed for conscious awareness. Additional pathways carry sensory information to brain stem nuclei as well as
subcortical nuclei. One of these subcortical nuclei, the amygdala,

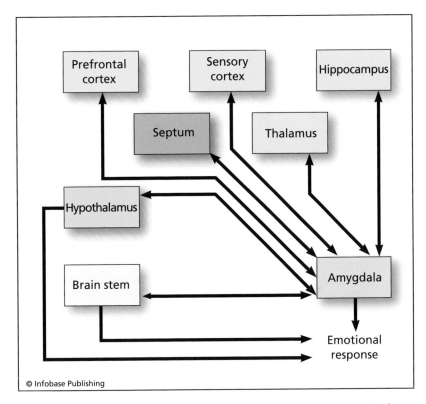

© Infobase Publishing

Figure 4.1 Information about a stimulus reaches the amygdala from
the sensory cortices and the thalamus. Memories about a stimulus stored in the hippocampus can help determine the amygdala's
response to that stimulus. In turn, the amygdala is involved in the
consolidation of new emotional memories. The prefrontal cortex not
only makes the final decision about how to react to a stimulus, but
also it can even inhibit the amygdala to keep it from overresponding.
Inputs by the amygdala to the hypothalamus and to the sympathetic
nervous system nuclei in the brain stem trigger the automatic physiological response to the stimulus.

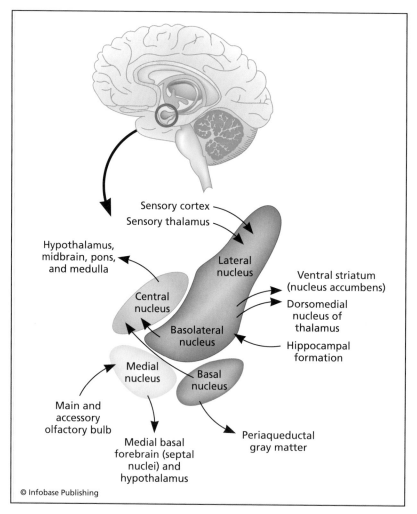

Figure 4.2 Some scientists divide the nuclei of the amygdala into four groups, as shown here. The lateral/basolateral nuclei have direct reciprocal connections with higher-order sensory cortices and the hippocampus and also send relays to the cortex through the thalamus and basal forebrain. Sensory information received by the basal nuclei from the lateral/basolateral nuclei is relayed to the periaqueductal gray matter and to other amygdaloid nuclei. The central nuclei receive information from the lateral/basolateral nuclei and from the brain stem and project to the lateral hypothalamus and the brain stem to regulate the autonomic nervous system. Medial nuclei receive primary olfactory information and relay it to the hypothalamus and medial basal forebrain.

is important in emotional expression and emotional recognition. The amygdala is actually a complex composed of multiple (about 12) nuclei, which are referred to by group and by location (Figure 4.2). The basolateral nucleus is the target of incoming sensory signals and is the most important input nucleus of the amygdala. Another group of nuclei, together called the **central nucleus**, is the primary target of the basolateral nucleus. The central nucleus is the major output area of the amygdala.

The central nucleus is considered the most important brain structure involved in emotional expression in response to threatening, or aversive, stimuli. Damage to this nucleus reduces or eliminates physiological responses and emotional behaviors. Since it supplies the central nucleus with sensory information, damage to the basolateral nucleus also produces this effect. Electrical stimulation of the central nucleus increases physiological and behavioral responses typical of the fear response.

SYMPATHETIC NERVOUS SYSTEM ACTIVATION

Output from the central nucleus of the amygdala to the hypothalamus is responsible for the physiological response to aversive stimuli. After it receives the signal from the amygdala, the **hypothalamus** sends out signals that activate the sympathetic nervous system. A group of neurons in the **paraventricular nucleus** of the hypothalamus sends messages down nerve fibers to sympathetic neurons located in the spinal cord. (There are also direct connections from the amygdala to the sympathetic neurons.) The sympathetic neurons in the spinal cord are **preganglionic neurons.** Preganglionic sympathetic neurons send messages to clusters of nerve cells called ganglia that are found in a chain along each side of the spinal column. The **postganglionic neurons** in the sympathetic ganglia then send messages to the organs and glands that they innervate.

Activation of the sympathetic nervous system results in an increase in blood pressure, heart rate, and the rate of breathing, which in turn results in the delivery of more oxygen to the brain and active muscles. The blood flow to the digestive tract and inactive muscles is reduced so that blood flow to the brain and active muscles can be increased. Perspiration increases so that the body will be cooled during the anticipated increase in activity. The pupils dilate so that far vision will be enhanced. Glucose is released from the liver, and fatty acids are released from **adipose tissue** (fat) to provide fuel for the brain and active muscles. (Glucose is the only fuel that can cross the blood-brain barrier except for **ketone bodies** produced by the liver during starvation. Ketone bodies are chemicals that are produced when fatty acids are broken down to form glucose.)

One of the glands innervated by the sympathetic nervous system is the **adrenal medulla**, which forms the core of the adrenal gland. In fact, the adrenal medulla is really a sympathetic ganglion. Its cells function as postganglionic neurons, but instead of sending out neural signals, they secrete hormones into the bloodstream. Activation of the sympathetic nervous system causes the adrenal medulla to secrete the hormones norepinephrine and epinephrine. Norepinephrine and epinephrine cause muscle cells to break stored nutrients into glucose for additional fuel. They also cause an increase of blood flow to the muscles.

NUCLEUS ACCUMBENS

Another subcortical structure, the nucleus accumbens, is primarily associated with positive emotions and is a critical component of the reward system. The nucleus accumbens is the target of neurons that use the neurotransmitter dopamine. These dopaminergic neurons reside in the **ventral tegmental area (VTA)**

Klüver-Bucy Syndrome

In 1937, Heinrich Klüver and Paul Bucy reported the first results of their study of the effects of damage to the temporal lobe on behavior. The set of behavioral symptoms they described in this first report have come to be known as the Klüver-Bucy Syndrome. Monkeys whose anterior temporal lobe had been removed bilaterally (on both sides) exhibited some bizarre behaviors. They were not afraid of things that monkeys are usually afraid of, such as people and snakes, nor did they display anger. This loss of normal emotions is called emotional blunting.

These monkeys put everything in sight, including inedible objects, into their mouths. Although they could see normally, they did not recognize objects that they saw. Klüver and Bucy called this symptom "psychic blindness" because they concluded that the monkeys put objects in their mouths to identify them because they could not do so visually. This mouthing of objects leads to hyperphagia, or overeating. Human patients with Klüver-Bucy Syndrome may have extreme weight gain if their diet is not monitored sufficiently.

Atypical sexual behaviors are also seen in monkeys with this disorder. They will make sexual advances to inanimate objects, animals of other species, and monkeys of the same sex. In humans—in which Klüver-Bucy Syndrome is rare—sexual activity is inappropriate and profuse. Klüver-Bucy Syndrome in humans usually results from herpes simplex encephalitis, head trauma, or surgical lesions.

Subsequent research has shown that damage to the amygdala is responsible for the emotional blunting seen in Klüver-Bucy Syndrome. However, additional damage to surrounding areas in the temporal lobe or to fibers that connect the amygdala with those areas is necessary to produce the full-blown syndrome.

of the midbrain. Dopamine is the neurotransmitter involved in the pleasure we experience from natural rewards. The taste of chocolate or sucrose (sugar) or the sight of an attractive face of the opposite sex will cause an increase in dopamine in the nucleus accumbens. Addictive drugs cause an abnormal increase in the level of dopamine released into the nucleus accumbens from the VTA (Figure 4.3).

Neuroimaging studies in humans have shown this activation of the nucleus accumbens in response to a number of drugs, including cocaine, heroin, and amphetamines. Activation of the nucleus accumbens after looking at photos of drug paraphernalia suggests that dopamine may be involved in the craving for drugs. Neurochemical studies in rats have shown that **secondary rewards**, or conditioned stimuli that have been repeatedly paired with drugs, food, or sex, will also cause the release of dopamine and the activation of the nucleus accumbens. Because of its connections to structures in both the limbic system and the motor system, the nucleus accumbens is considered an interface between these two systems.

PERIAQUEDUCTAL GRAY
Signals from the central nucleus of the amygdala are also sent to brain areas that are responsible for emotional behavioral responses. There are inputs from the central amygdaloid nucleus and the hypothalamus to an area in the brain stem called the **periaqueductal gray**. The periaqueductal gray surrounds the **cerebral aqueduct**, the narrow duct that connects the third and fourth ventricles. This area consists primarily of neuronal cell bodies, or **gray matter**, hence its name. One of the functions of the periaqueductal gray is to activate motor responses to emotional stimuli. These responses fall into three categories: fight, flight, or freezing.

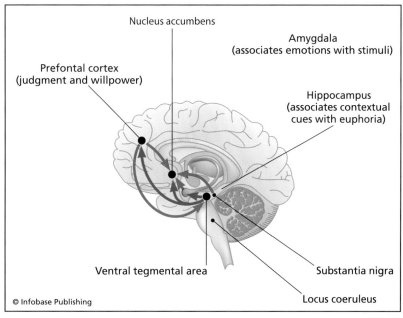

Nucleus accumbens

Amygdala
(associates emotions with stimuli)

Prefontal cortex
(judgment and willpower)

Hippocampus
(associates contextual
cues with euphoria)

Ventral tegmental area

Substantia nigra

Locus coeruleus

© Infobase Publishing

Figure 4.3 Drugs of abuse increase the release of dopamine from neurons of the ventral tegmental area that synapse in the nucleus accumbens. Some addictive drugs have actions in other brain structures as well. Depicted here are the basic dopaminergic pathways from the ventral tegmental area to the nucleus accumbens, prefrontal cortex, and amygdala.

PREFRONTAL CORTEX

Whereas the amygdala appears to be the most important structure in generating an emotional response, the **prefrontal cortex** is important in regulating that response (Figure 4.4). Inhibitory projections from the ventral prefrontal cortex to the amygdala suppress inappropriate emotional responses and allow voluntary control of emotional expression. Moral judgments and decisions regarding risk versus reward are guided by emotional reactions. Damage to the ventral prefrontal cortex has been shown to impair these decisions. Impulsive violence due to faulty emotional regulation is also believed to be a result of impairment of the ventral prefrontal cortex.

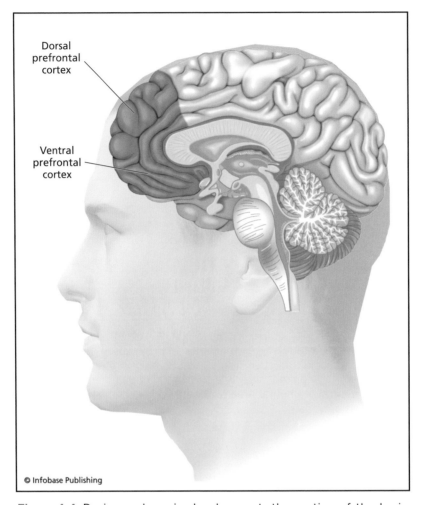

Dorsal
prefrontal
cortex

Ventral
prefrontal
cortex

© Infobase Publishing

Figure 4.4 During embryonic development, the portion of the brain containing the future cerebral hemispheres grows into a C-shaped structure, which folds down to the diencephalon, to which it eventually fuses. This causes parts of the cerebral hemispheres, such as the ventral prefrontal cortex, to lie on the "underside" of the brain. The prefrontal cortex is important in judgment and in the control of emotions.

The famous story of Phineas Gage illustrates the importance of the prefrontal cortex. Phineas Gage was a railroad construction crew foreman who was industrious, serious, dependable, and well liked. In 1848, Gage rammed an explosive charge into a hole in a rock with a steel rod. The blasting powder exploded unexpectedly and sent the steel rod through Gage's cheek and brain and out through the top of his head. Later analysis of the trajectory, or path, of the steel rod determined that his entire orbitofrontal cortex had been destroyed. After Gage recovered from the injury, he was no longer the same man as before. He was now irresponsible, childish, impulsive, and profane. Unable to return to his construction job, Gage drove coaches and worked in livery stables and even appeared in New York at P.T. Barnum's museum.

Another example of the importance of the prefrontal cortex is the devastating effects caused by a surgical procedure that was introduced in the 1930s by Egas Moniz. Known as the **prefrontal lobotomy**, this procedure quickly became popular as a treatment for schizophrenia. Using various forms of the procedure, physicians destroyed the connections between the prefrontal cortex and subcortical structures. The most famous example of the technique was the ice pick lobotomy, which was introduced by neurologist Walter Freeman in 1945. With this particular version of the procedure, a modified ice pick was inserted underneath the upper eyelid. A tap with a hammer sent the pick through the bone, and a semicircular turn of the instrument cut through nerve fibers. Rosemary Kennedy, the sister of President John F. Kennedy, was one of the victims of this procedure. As a result of the harmful effects of the procedure, she had to be institutionalized until her death at age 86.

Although the prefrontal lobotomy procedure relieved anxiety and calmed unruly patients, its harmful effects soon became apparent. Infections and fatalities were reported. Autopsies sometimes revealed the destruction of large areas of brain tissue. Many of those who survived lost not only the negative emotions they were treated for but also desirable emotions. Often they became impulsive and irresponsible and were unable to hold a job. The adverse effects were so great that the procedure was abandoned by the mid-1950s. Ironically, Egas Moniz had been awarded a Nobel Prize in 1949 for his introduction of the infamous technique.

■ **Learn more about the contents of this chapter** Search the Internet for *sympathetic nervous system*, *adrenal gland*, and *reward pathway*.

5 | Emotion and Cognition

Just as there is intricate interplay between the nervous system and the endocrine and immune systems, there is also intricate interplay between the cognitive, emotional, sensory, and motor functions of the brain. In this chapter, we will look at how emotions affect cognition—how the emotional brain affects the thinking brain. We will find that emotions are an integral part of the overall cognitive functioning of an individual and play many roles in both conscious and unconscious experiences.

EMOTIONAL RECOGNITION

An important part of the communication of emotions is the recognition, or perception, of emotions. In other words, emotional expression is on the sending end and **emotional recognition** is on the receiving end of emotional communication. The same general brain areas are important in both expression and recognition of emotion. There is also a certain amount of **brain lateralization** in emotional recognition, with the right hemisphere being more important overall. This varies, however, between structures within the hemispheres.

Stanford University neurologist Ralph Adolphs and his colleagues did a study in which they used subjects who had localized damage to a number of different brain areas. The researchers tested the subjects on their ability to recognize facial expressions for the six basic emotions. Their results showed that damage in the right primary and secondary somatosensory cortices produced the greatest impairment in recognition of emotion from facial expressions. (Remember that the somatosensory cortices receive and process information from the bodily senses.) In addition, they found that recognition of fear expressions was also impaired by damage to the right anterior temporal lobe. Remember that the anterior temporal lobe is where the amygdala and surrounding structures are located. Their analysis of the data also showed that damage in the right frontoparietal cortex caused impairment in the recognition of all six basic emotions.

Lesions of the amygdala caused by surgery or degenerative disease impair a person's ability to recognize emotional facial expressions, particularly fear expressions. Unlike the recognition of emotion from facial expressions, recognition of emotion from tone of voice does not appear to be impaired by amygdala lesions. Neuroimaging studies in normal subjects have shown large increases in amygdala activity while viewing photos of faces with fear expressions. Happy expressions elicited small increases in activity.

Other studies have shown the prefrontal cortex to be important in emotional recognition as well. Blood flow in the prefrontal cortex was observed in one study to increase on both sides but more so on the left side during the comprehension of emotion from the meaning of words. This may be due to the greater involvement of the left hemisphere in language. It increased only in the right prefrontal cortex during emotional recognition by the tone of voice.

The cingulate cortex may also be involved in the emotional recognition of facial expressions. In one study, photographs depicting a negative emotional scene tended to produce more activation of the right cingulate gyrus. Another study found that happy faces activated the left cingulate gyrus.

EMOTIONAL LEARNING

Physiological and behavioral responses to aversive stimuli can be learned. If a neutral stimulus such as a tone or light repeatedly occurs just before the aversive stimulus occurs, eventually the neutral stimulus will elicit a similar, but weaker, response without the aversive stimulus being present. This type of response is called a **conditioned emotional response**. The once-neutral stimulus becomes a conditioned stimulus by its association with the aversive stimulus (the unconditioned stimulus). The conditioned emotional response is a reflexlike reaction to the conditioned stimulus that predicts the occurrence of the aversive stimulus. Rats will stop pressing a lever for food, for example, if a tone comes on that predicts a small electrical shock.

Conditioned fear is thought to underlie human **phobias**. (A phobia is a strong irrational fear of things such as spiders or heights.) The most famous example of a conditioned emotional response is a study conducted in the early twentieth century by psychologist John Watson and his graduate student Rosalie Rayner at Johns Hopkins University. In this experiment, "Little Albert," who was a well-adjusted 11-month-old boy, was allowed to play with a white rat. In the beginning of the experiment, Albert was not afraid of the white rat. However, after the researchers struck a steel bar, making a loud noise whenever he approached the rat, Albert became afraid of the rat. Not only was he afraid of the rat, but he also feared any object that was furry and white, such as a fur coat or a Santa Claus mask. Unfortunately, Little Albert moved away, and the researchers were unable to reverse this learned, or conditioned, fear reaction.

Lesion studies have shown that both the basolateral and the central nuclei of the amygdala are important for the formation

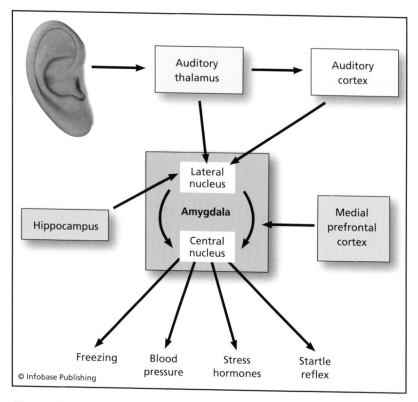

Figure 5.1 Fear conditioning to an auditory stimulus involves the short route from the auditory thalamus to the amygdala. If either the auditory thalamus or the lateral nucleus of the amygdala is lesioned, fear conditioning to an auditory stimulus (such as a tone) will not occur. Conditioning to contextual stimuli requires an intact hippocampus and amygdala. Lesions of the central nucleus of the amygdala will block both the behavioral and physiological components of the fear response.

of a conditioned emotional response and for its expression after conditioning (Figure 5.1). Sensory information comes to the amygdala from the thalamus by both direct and indirect paths. For example, an auditory stimulus goes first to the medial geniculate nucleus of the thalamus before going to the amygdala. The auditory stimulus also travels from the thalamus to the auditory cortex, which in turn sends information to the amygdala. It is thought that the direct route from the thalamus to the amygdala allows the amygdala to quickly identify the emotional significance of a stimulus.

Fear conditioning to the **context**, or environment, in which a fear-inducing stimulus is encountered also occurs. This is called **contextual fear conditioning** and involves both the amygdala and the hippocampus. Rats learn to associate not only a tone or other neutral stimulus with an aversive stimulus such as footshock but also with the cage (context) in which it occurred. Even without a conditioned stimulus, a rat will develop a fear of a particular cage in which it receives footshocks.

You can probably think of an example of an environment in which you feel uneasy or afraid for no apparent reason. This may be a dentist's office or a doctor's office for some people. It could be a swimming pool for someone who has had a near-drowning experience. Or it could be a sharp turn in the highway for someone who has been involved in an accident. If you have ever been stranded in a broken elevator, you may feel uneasy whenever you step into an elevator or are confined in a narrow space. All of us have had experiences that cause our amygdalas to sound an alarm when contextual or other stimuli recall these experiences.

EMOTION AND ATTENTION

The sense organs are constantly bombarded by a multitude of stimuli from the internal and external environments. **Selective attention** is the cognitive function that allows us to attend (pay attention) to stimuli that are relevant or important at any given time. Attention enhances important or relevant stimuli while eliminating distracting ones. For example, as you read this book, you are focusing on one sentence at a time and ignoring the rest of the page. When you are riding your bike or driving a car, you are more aware of the traffic and road conditions than you are of the landscape passing by. At a party, you tune in to conversations you are engaged in and tune out many other voices and sounds.

There is a difference of opinion among scientists as to the exact brain mechanisms involved, but it is generally agreed that there are important interactions between emotion and attention. Some scientists believe that stimuli with emotional content have to compete with neutral stimuli to gain access to conscious awareness through selective attention. Other scientists believe that emotion-laden stimuli travel a faster subcortical route to the thalamus and then the amygdala to be processed without conscious awareness. According to this view, the amygdala then signals the prefrontal cortex, which gives priority to processing and reacting to these stimuli.

Visual backward-masking is a research technique in which a stimulus is presented briefly on a screen and is followed immediately by another stimulus. The first stimulus is called the target stimulus, and the second stimulus is called the mask. This is done so quickly that the subject has no conscious awareness of the target stimulus being presented. Using the PET neuroimaging technique, neuropsychiatrist Raymond Dolan and his colleagues at the University College London found that the amygdala activates in response to the presentation of fearful faces as target stimuli.

Processes that occur within the brain without reaching conscious awareness are said to be automatic, or possess **automaticity**. Automaticity is one of the key features of skill learning. Once we have learned how to ice-skate or play the piano, for example, we no longer have to think about each movement. At this point, skilled movements are smoother and faster. Reading is another skill that becomes automatic after it is well learned. Automaticity in the processing of emotion-laden stimuli would have the same advantages of speed and efficiency. It could mean the difference between life and death in a threatening situation.

EMOTION AND MEMORY

If you relax and let your mind wander back through time, which memories are most likely to come to mind? Your first day of school, your favorite pet, a fun-filled vacation, or your first date may be among the things that come to mind. Our most prominent and lasting memories are packed with emotion-laden stimuli. Why is it that **emotional memories**, as they are sometimes called, are so well preserved? Is it because they are recalled more often so that they are well rehearsed? Or is it because there is something different about the way they are stored in the brain?

The amygdala participates in the **consolidation**, or storage, of emotional memories. It is thought that the actual storage place for memories is located in different places in the brain for different types of memories. Some scientists believe that memories are stored in neuronal circuits within the brain areas that initially process the information after it enters the brain. For example, visual memories are thought to be stored in visual association cortex and auditory memories in auditory association cortex, and so on.

Although consolidation of fear conditioning may take place in the amygdala itself, most of the amygdala's effect on memory consolidation appears to involve its projections to other brain areas. These areas include the hippocampus, the nucleus accumbens, the caudate nucleus, and cortical areas, particularly the orbitofrontal cortex and the insular cortex.

Human studies of the amygdala have confirmed the animal studies that indicate the importance of the amygdala in consolidation of emotional memories. Long-term memory of emotion-laden material is impaired in patients who have selective damage of the amygdala. Neuroimaging studies (PET and fMRI) in subjects with intact amygdalas show that the amygdala activity while viewing emotionally arousing material is correlated with long-term memory of the material. One of these studies used emotionally arousing, pleasant material. Most studies of the amygdala have focused on aversive stimuli, but it is becoming apparent that the amygdala influences the enhancement of consolidation of emotional arousal produced by positive stimuli as well.

EMOTIONAL INTELLIGENCE
Early intelligence researchers, including David Wechsler in the 1940s, recognized the importance of noncognitive components

Flashbulb Memories

Flashbulb memories are memories with "photographic" quality of an event of great emotional significance. They were first described by Roger Brown and James Kulik at Harvard University in 1977. Most of us can remember what we were doing when we heard of the hijacked planes striking the Twin Towers of the World Trade Center in New York City on September 11, 2001. Many baby boomers remember where they were when they heard the news about John F. Kennedy's assassination. Most of us have one or more of these memories that seem as if they happened yesterday.

Flashbulb memories are very vivid and accompanied by a great amount of confidence in their accuracy. There is a difference of opinion among scientists, however, as to whether they are a special type of memory. Scientists like Joseph LeDoux at New York University would refer to the rise in epinephrine that accompanies an emotional event and point out that epinephrine has a positive effect on memory consolidation. To test this idea, of intelligence. Robert Thorndike wrote about "social intelligence" in the late 1930s. However, the focus of intelligence research shifted to cognitive components of intelligence until Howard Gardner wrote about "multiple intelligences" in 1983.

In the late 1980s, John Mayer and Peter Salovey began their research on the topic of **emotional intelligence** (Figure 5.2). The model proposed by Mayer and Salovey views emotional intelligence as consisting of four "branches" or areas: 1) perceiving one's own emotions and those of others, 2) understanding the messages and potential actions associated with those emotions, 3) facilitation of thought by the use of emotions, and 4) management or regulation of one's own emotions and those of

James McGaugh and Larry Cahill of the University of California-Irvine conducted a study in which one group of subjects read a neutral story and another group read an emotional story. Half of the subjects from each group were then injected with a placebo, and half were injected with a drug that blocks the receptors that epinephrine acts on. Subjects that received the placebo and read the emotional story remembered details much better than those who received placebo or the blocking drug and read the neutral story. They also remembered the details better than the subjects who received the blocking drug and read the emotional story.

Other scientists, however, have contended that flashbulb memories are no more accurate than other memories, that they are just rehearsed more often. These scientists point out that errors could be added due to discussion with others or seeing the event repeated on the media. Ulric Neisser suggested that flashbulb memories occur when a moment in our lives links with history and that is why we remember them so well.

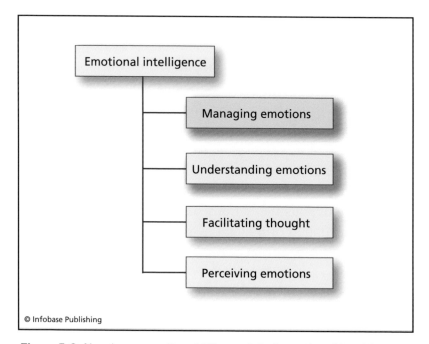

Figure 5.2 Now known as the ability model of emotional intelligence, Mayer and Salovey's model viewed emotional intelligence as consist- ing of four sets of abilities, ranked in this diagram in order of com- plexity. Simple abilities involved in recognizing emotions of oneself and others and in accurately expressing emotions are represented in the lowest branch. Next in complexity is the use of emotions to guide reasoning and facilitate thought. Understanding emotions, their differences, similarities, and patterns, and the situations they relate to is the next-highest level. Managing one's emotions so as to engage or disengage them as appropriate and the ability to elicit desired emotions from others is considered the highest ability level of emotional intelligence.

others, including groups of people. Mayer and Salovey named a set of emotional abilities or skills related to each of these areas. They believed that, based on these skills, emotional intelligence could be measured, much like cognitive intelligence is measured with intelligence quotient (IQ) tests.

In 1995, journalist Daniel Goleman popularized the new field of study in his book *Emotional Intelligence: Why It Can Matter*

More Than IQ. Goleman expanded Mayer and Salovey's model and reviewed a number of other studies. Unlike Mayer and Salovey, Goleman proposed that one's emotional intelligence can predict one's success in life.

The theory of emotional intelligence is still a subject of debate among scientists as to its scientific validity and how to measure it. It remains to be seen how well it will withstand the rigors of scientific analysis.

■ **Learn more about the contents of this chapter** Search the Internet for *emotional intelligence, conditioned emotional response,* and *emotional memory.*

6 | The Stress Response

THE BEGINNINGS OF STRESS RESEARCH

There was an increasing awareness of the influence of emotional factors and the "pace of life" on one's health during the nineteenth century. It was not until the early twentieth century, however, that the concept of stress was formally introduced and subsequently became the focus of a new field of research. The two most famous early pioneers in stress-related research were Walter Cannon and Hans Selye.

Cannon and his colleagues at Harvard University observed profound physiological changes that occurred in response to the secretions of the adrenal glands. He further observed that these secretions increased in response to emotional excitement. Cannon contended that the sympathetic nervous system is responsible for mobilizing the body's defensive forces during times of intense fear or rage. In 1929, he coined the term *fight-or-flight response* to describe this emergency response (Figure 6.1). He discovered a neurochemical that he called sympathin that was produced by sympathetic nerve endings and was later identified as norepinephrine. Cannon also coined the term *homeostasis* in 1932 to describe the steady state maintained by the body's physiological processes. According to Cannon, it was the job of the sympathetic nervous system to help maintain this stable internal environment.

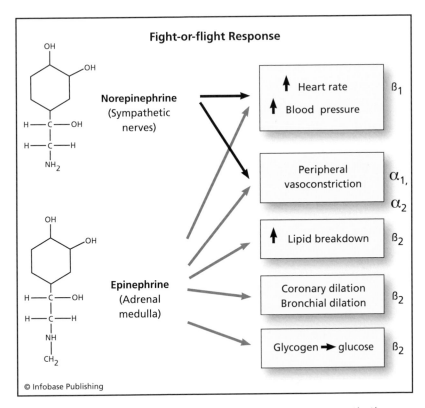

Figure 6.1 During the fight-or-flight response, the sympathetic nervous system is activated, resulting in the release of norepinephrine from sympathetic nerves and of epinephrine from the adrenal gland. Norepinephrine is also released from the adrenal gland but in much smaller quantities. Physiological effects that prepare the body for an emergency situation are shown here. The catecholamine receptor subtype involved in each action is shown in the far right column.

In 1934, Hans Selye, then at McGill University in Montreal, was attempting to discover a new hormone by giving rats a daily injection of ovarian extract. He hoped to observe changes that did not occur with the sex hormones known at that time and that might indicate the presence of another sex hormone. When he dissected the rats after a few days of these injections, he discovered that they had enlarged adrenals and shrunken spleen, thymus, and lymph nodes as well as gastro-intestinal ulcers. At first, he believed that he had discovered a new ovarian hormone. He subsequently discovered that injection of extracts of numerous other organs, including the kidney, spleen, and pituitary gland, as well as the preservative formalin, produced the same symptoms. Eventually, he concluded that what he had witnessed was a nonspecific response of the body to "noxious agents."

In his 1936 paper, Selye dubbed the set of symptoms he had observed in his rat experiments the **general adaptation syndrome**. He proposed that it consisted of three stages: alarm, resistance, and exhaustion. During the alarm stage, which was equivalent to Cannon's fight-or-flight response, the body mobilized its resources to respond to the noxious agent. If the noxious challenge continued, the body built up a resistance to it during the resistance stage. Unless the body was able to overcome the influence of the noxious agent, the exhaustion stage would ensue as the body's resources were exhausted, and death would result.

Because of his contribution to the field over a period of 50 years, most of it spent at the University of Montreal, Selye is commonly known as the father of stress research. As is always true in science, however, many of the discoveries that were incorporated into his ongoing research came from the cumulative work of other scientists. By the time of Selye's death in 1982, the neuroendocrine pathway from the brain to the adrenal gland had been traced. In *The Nature of Stress*, finished shortly before his death, Selye described the neuroendocrine underpinnings of his general adaptation syndrome. A second major pathway, the **hypothalamic-pituitary-adrenal (HPA) axis**, had now been added to our understanding of the fight-or-flight response.

THE STRESS RESPONSE

During the stress response, the amygdala sounds the alarm and signals the hypothalamus, which activates both the sympathetic nervous system and the HPA axis (Figure 6.2). In addition, the amygdala activates the noradrenergic (norepinephrine) system by signaling the **locus coeruleus** in the pons. That nucleus then discharges norepinephrine from its widespread projections in the brain. This has an activating effect on the brain and increases alertness.

The sympathetic nervous system not only releases the neurotransmitter norpinephrine from its postganglionic nerve endings, but also activates the adrenal medulla, which produces the hormones epinephrine and norepinephrine. Since chemical messengers (neurotransmitters) travel between neurons to activate the sympathetic nervous system, that chain of responses is much faster than those of the HPA axis. The chemical messengers that activate the HPA axis are hormones that travel through the bloodstream. Consequently, their actions are somewhat slower.

Pituitary Gland

Hormones of the HPA axis are produced by the **pituitary gland**, the hypothalamus, and the adrenal glands. At the base of the hypothalamus is a small protuberance called the **median eminence**, which connects to the **infundibulum**, or stalk, of the pituitary gland. The pituitary gland resembles a small fig suspended from the base of the brain in front of the brain stem. It sits inside a bony socket in the skull underneath it. The pituitary gland consists of two lobes, an anterior lobe and a posterior lobe. Connected to the hypothalamus by the infundibulum, the posterior lobe, or **neurohypophysis**, is considered part of the brain because of its embryonic origin. The anterior lobe, or

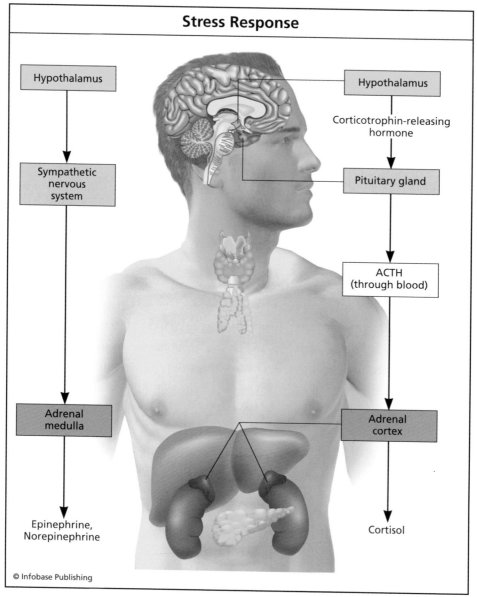

Figure 6.2 When activated by a signal from the amygdala, the hypothalamus activates the sympathetic nervous system and the HPA axis. Activated by the sympathetic nervous system, the adrenal medulla releases epinephrine and nor-epinephrine into the bloodstream. Corticotrophin-releasing hormone released by the hypothalamus causes the pituitary gland to release ACTH, which causes the adrenal cortex to release cortisol into the bloodstream.

adenohypophysis, is considered an endocrine gland because it synthesizes a number of hormones and secretes them into the bloodstream. Its embryonic origin is also different from that of the neurohypophysis.

Hypothalamus

Axons from the paraventricular and supraoptic nuclei of the hypothalamus extend down into the neurohypophysis and release the **neurohormones** vasopressin and oxytocin near capillaries in the posterior lobe. (Neurohormones, as their name implies, are hormones that are secreted by neurons.) These hormones enter the capillaries and are carried into the general bloodstream.

All other hormones secreted by hypothalamic neurons are secreted from nerve endings near a network of capillaries in the median eminence and the adjacent portion of the infundibulum. **Hypophyseal portal vessels,** the small veins and venules that these capillaries drain into, course through the infundibular stalk into the anterior lobe of the pituitary and empty into another network of capillaries found in the adenohypophysis. Some of these neurohormones are carried from there into the general circulation to act on targets elsewhere in the body. Others either stimulate or inhibit the production of hormones by the endocrine cells of the adenohypophysis.

Adrenal Gland

Perched atop each kidney, much like a little cap, the **adrenal gland** consists of an outer layer called the **adrenal cortex** and a central core called the adrenal medulla. The cortex and medulla of the adrenal gland have different embryological origins. Because it developed from the **neural crest,** which separates from the central nervous system to become the peripheral nervous system, the adrenal medulla is actually part of the sympathetic nervous system. When the sympathetic nervous system is activated, the adrenal medulla releases the stress hormones epinephrine and norepinephrine into the bloodstream. The adrenal cortex produces several hormones, which include **cortisol**, the primary **glucocorticoid** in humans. The adrenal medulla is activated by acetylcholine released from the nerve endings of sympathetic preganglionic neurons, whereas the release of cortisol from the adrenal cortex is triggered by the hormone **adrenocorticotropic hormone** (ACTH), which reaches it by way of the bloodstream.

The HPA Axis

Corticotrophin-releasing hormone is produced by neurons in the paraventricular nucleus of the hypothalamus and carried in the hypophyseal portal system to the adenohypophysis, where it stimulates the production of adrenocorticotrophic hormone (ACTH). After entering the general circulation, ACTH travels in the bloodstream to the adrenal glands, where it stimulates the adrenal cortex to produce cortisol. This hormonal pathway from the hypothalamus to the pituitary to the adrenal cortex is known as the hypothalamic-pituitary-adrenocortical axis.

FEEDBACK CONTROL OF CORTISOL

Cortisol is produced continuously in a daily rhythmic cycle called a **diurnal rhythm**. Peak levels of cortisol occur about an hour before waking in humans, usually between 6:00 to 8:00 in the morning. The lowest levels of cortisol occur in the evening. (Rats, like other nocturnal animals, are active at night. Corticosterone, their primary glucocorticoid hormone, peaks in the evening an hour or two before the rats' activity cycle begins.) Cortisol is normally secreted at the rate of 10 to 30 mg per day in humans, but this rate can be increased as much as tenfold during stress. When blood levels of the hormone rise to a certain level, a negative feedback mechanism kicks in to restore normal levels.

There are cortisol receptors on practically every cell in the body, including neurons. A high density of cortisol receptors is found in the hypothalamus, and an even higher density is found in the hippocampus. Higher levels of cortisol act at the level of the hypothalamus to reduce the production of corticotrophin-releasing hormone and at the level of the pituitary gland to reduce the production of ACTH. The hippocampus regulates the daily levels of cortisol and is thought to participate in the feedback control of the hypothalamic-pituitary-adrenocortical axis during stress. Exactly what the role of the hippocampus is in this process has not yet been determined.

EFFECTS OF CORTISOL

Because it is synthesized in a series of steps from cholesterol, cortisol is classified as a steroid hormone. Steroid hormones are fat soluble and can pass through the cell membrane, which is composed primarily of fat. They then bind to their specific receptors inside the cell. Cortisol binds to its receptors either in the cytoplasm or the nucleus of the cell (Figure 6.3). If it binds to a cytoplasmic receptor, the receptor-hormone complex is transported to the nucleus, where it binds to DNA.

A certain level of cortisol is necessary for normal functioning. Either too little or too much cortisol can affect health adversely. The main job of cortisol is to make sure there is enough glucose in the bloodstream. It does that by stimulating the breakdown of stored fat into fatty acids and glycerol, promoting the breakdown of muscle protein into amino acids, and stimulating the liver enzymes responsible for converting amino acids and fatty acids to glucose. Glycerol from the breakdown of stored fat can also be converted into glucose by the liver. In addition, cortisol inhibits the secretion of insulin, which is necessary for glucose

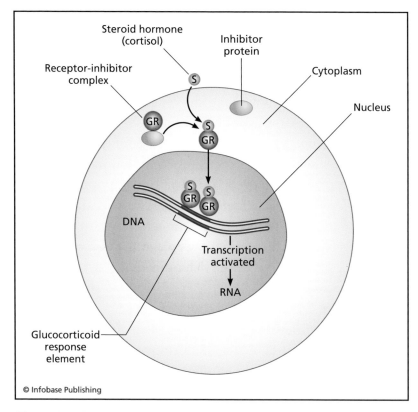

Steroid hormone
(cortisol)

Inhibitor
protein

Receptor-inhibitor
complex

Cytoplasm

Nucleus

DNA

Transcription
activated

RNA

Glucocorticoid
response
element

© Infobase Publishing

Figure 6.3 Once cortisol has bound to a glucocorticoid receptor in the cytoplasm, the resulting receptor complex travels to the nucleus of the cell, where it binds to a glucocorticoid response element in the DNA. This causes RNA for the target gene to be produced (transcribed), which in turn causes an increase in the production of the protein for which the target gene encodes. Inhibitory proteins have been identified that can bind to the glucocorticoid receptor complex and prevent it from binding to its response element.

to enter all cells except neurons. This decrease in insulin makes a greater portion of the glucose in the bloodstream available to neurons during stress.

Cortisol works with norepinephrine to maintain normal blood pressure and to maintain the tone of the blood vessels and the integrity of the endothelium (lining) of the blood vessels. It also stimulates the synthesis of norepinephrine and epinephrine in the adrenal medulla, as well as that of the receptors to which these hormones bind. Cortisol facilitates kidney function by stimulating blood flow in the glomeruli, which are tufts of capillaries through which liquids and soluble solids are filtered to be further processed into urine.

Numerous maturational events in the fetus that prepare it for birth are regulated by cortisol. Lung maturation and the production of **lung surfactant** are stimulated by cortisol. (Lung surfactant lowers surface tension so that air is absorbed more easily. It also prevents the blockage of airways by water droplets.) Cortisol stimulates the production of glucose in the fetal liver and its storage as glycogen. This is a way of storing energy for the fetus until it has its first feeding. Cortisol also facilitates the maturation of the gastrointestinal tract, central nervous system, skin, and retina.

ADDISON'S DISEASE

What happens if the body does not produce enough cortisol? **Addison's disease,** or **hypocortisolism,** is the name for a disorder in which too little cortisol is produced by the adrenal cortex. This may be due to a problem at the level of the adrenal gland (**primary adrenal insufficiency**) or from production of too little ACTH by the pituitary gland (**secondary adrenal insufficiency.**) Addison's disease afflicts about 1 in 100,000 people.

Symptoms of Addison's disease, which usually begin gradually, include weight loss, loss of appetite, muscle weakness, and chronic fatigue that gets worse. Nausea, vomiting, and diarrhea occur about 50% of the time. Dizziness or fainting due to low blood pressure that worsens upon standing can also occur. Hyperpigmentation, or darkening, of the skin on scars, at folds in the skin, over the joints, and on the lips is characteristic. Irritability, depression, salt craving, and hypoglycemia may occur.

A stressful event or an accident can cause an **addisonian crisis**, which may be fatal if left untreated. Sudden penetrating pain in the abdomen, legs, or lower back, followed by severe vomiting and diarrhea with dehydration, low blood pressure, and subsequent loss of consciousness are characteristic of an addisonian crisis. Immediate treatment with injections of saline and glucocorticoids is required.

Chronic Fatigue Syndrome

Chronic fatigue syndrome is a chronic debilitating illness that is somewhat mysterious because there is no diagnostic laboratory test for it and no prescribed treatment strategy that seems to work for everyone. A diagnosis of chronic fatigue syndrome is usually arrived at after excluding other illnesses that share one or more of its symptoms. The current criteria for a diagnosis of chronic fatigue syndrome include the presence of severe chronic fatigue that has lasted for at least 6 months. In addition, 4 or more of the following symptoms must be present: sleep that does not refresh; tiredness that lasts more than 24 hours after exertion; tender lymph nodes; sore throat; multijoint pain that is not accompanied by redness or swelling; muscle pain; headaches that are different in type, severity, or pattern than any experienced before; and problems with concentration or short-term memory, sometimes referred to as "brain fog." Symptoms worsen after either psychological or physiological stress.

Although there are probably many factors that interact to produce the symptoms of this illness, most scientists agree that it is a stress-related disorder. Both Addison's disease and the removal of both adrenal glands result in low blood levels of cortisol. In addition, both of those conditions result

CUSHING'S SYNDROME

Cushing's syndrome, or **hypercortisolism**, affects 10 to 15 per million people yearly, so it is relatively rare. Usual symptoms are obesity of the upper body, an increase in neck fat, a rounded face, and a thinning of legs and arms. The skin becomes thin and fragile, bruises easily, and heals slowly. Stretch marks of a purplish pink color may be present on the abdomen,

in debilitating fatigue. Therefore, it is believed that one of the underlying causes of chronic fatigue syndrome is an imbalance somewhere in the HPA axis.

A number of scientists have examined various components of the HPA axis, from the hypothalamus all the way to the adrenal cortex. For example, Jens Gaab and his research team found that people who have chronic fatigue syndrome have a lower ACTH level than normal, both before and after psychological and physical stressors as well as after a series of insulin injections that challenges the HPA axis. Anthony Clearne and his colleagues measured the level of cortisol in the urine of chronic fatigue syndrome patients over a 24-hour period and found that it was lower than normal.

Most scientists believe that there is a problem either at the level of the hypothalamus, where corticotrophin-releasing hormone is produced, or at the level of the pituitary gland, where ACTH is produced. Bruce McEwen of Rockefeller University believes that a sluggish HPA axis that does not produce enough cortisol allows an increase in inflammatory cytokines (immune system chemical messengers). In other words, a sluggish HPA axis takes the brakes off the immune system, with disastrous consequences.

buttocks, arms, thighs, and breasts. Weakened bones may result in fractures from everyday activities. Muscle weakness, severe fatigue, high blood sugar, and high blood pressure are the usual symptoms. Anxiety, irritability, and depression are common symptoms. Excess hair on the face, chest, thighs, and abdomen is usually present in women with the disorder. Decreased fertility and diminished or absent sexual desire is usually present in men.

Most cases of Cushing's syndrome are caused by benign tumors of the pituitary gland that produce large amounts of ACTH, which in turn cause the levels of cortisol to increase. **Ectopic ACTH syndrome** is caused by a tumor located somewhere other than the pituitary gland. Cushing's syndrome can also result from the extended use of glucocorticoids to treat various diseases. Tumors of the adrenal glands, usually noncancerous, are another cause of Cushing's syndrome.

Either overproduction or underproduction of cortisol can have drastic effects on one's health. However, cortisol produced in normal amounts is essential to life and the maintenance of good health. Rats whose adrenal glands are removed will die if they are not given synthetic glucocorticoids. Addison's disease patients also require supplementation with glucocorticoids.

■ **Learn more about the contents of this chapter**   Search the Internet for *glucocorticoid*, *neurohormone*, and *diurnal rhythm*.

7 | Stress and Health

Stress research has revealed the important role that the stress response plays in health and disease. As a result of this research, it has been discovered that stress can cause or make worse a number of chronic or degenerative diseases. Its effect on the immune system and the endocrine system can have far-reaching consequences on the rest of the body. Stress hormones produced during both acute stress and chronic stress have important health effects. The combined effects of cortisol and the catecholamine hormones range on a continuum from promoting health to being deadly.

STRESS AND THE CARDIOVASCULAR SYSTEM

When the stress response is activated, the sympathetic nervous system releases norepinephrine at nerve endings in the heart and on the blood vessels. Some of the norepinephrine released from sympathetic nerve endings enters the circulation. As a result of stimulation by the sympathetic nervous system, the adrenal medulla releases norepinephrine and epinephrine into the bloodstream. (Epinephrine makes up 80% of adrenal catecholamines, and norepinephrine the other 20%.) Since epinephrine is the primary output of the adrenal medulla, most of the norepinephrine in the bloodstream comes from sympathetic nerve endings.

There are two types of receptors to which norepinephrine and epinephrine bind. These hormones activate beta-adrenergic receptors in the heart and alpha-adrenergic receptors in the blood vessels. (Catecholamine receptors are called **adrenergic** receptors.) This causes the heart to beat harder and faster and the blood vessels to constrict. Together, this causes the blood pressure to rise. Cortisol enhances the effects of the catecholamines.

This rise in blood pressure is part of the fight-or-flight response that helps prepare the body for action. It is beneficial during acute (temporary) stress, but if it is repeated too often it can cause wear and tear on the heart and blood vessels. Chronic and repeated increases of blood pressure can lead to **hypertension**, or high blood pressure. This causes the blood vessels to weaken over time.

Small tears, or lesions, can occur in the walls of the larger arteries, especially where they branch. An inflammatory response occurs at the sites of these tiny lesions. Deposits of plaque attach to them and cause the arteries to become stiffer. These plaque deposits may be composed of immune cells attracted to the lesion, clumped platelets, and fatty substances such as cholesterol. These changes in the lining of blood vessels are known as **atherosclerosis**, or "hardening of the arteries." A buildup of plaque causes the lumen (central cavity) of the arteries to narrow (Figure 7.1).

Blood clots can form at the narrowed branches of arteries or around chunks of plaque that break away from the artery walls. Epinephrine stimulates an increase in **fibrinogen**, which makes platelets more likely to stick together. This is designed to protect the body during acute stress by reducing the flow of blood from wounds or breaks in the skin. A chronic increase in fibrinogen increases the risk of clot formation. If

Atherosclerosis

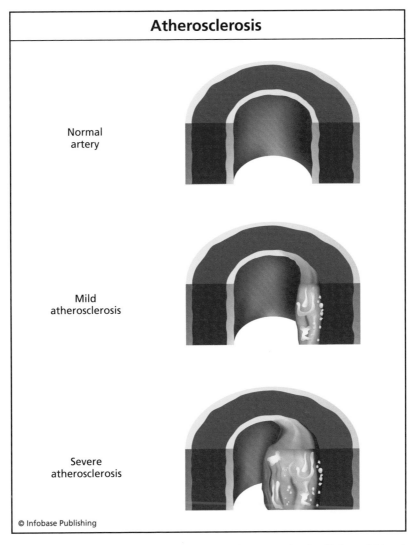

Normal
artery

Mild
atherosclerosis

Severe
atherosclerosis

© Infobase Publishing

Figure 7.1 Atherosclerosis begins with tiny tears in the lining of blood vessels. This usually occurs in locations where the blood hits the artery wall with greater force, as in the large vessels leaving the heart and at branches in vessels. Lymphocytes rush to the scene and become part of the buildup that gradually narrows the lumen of the artery. Other components of atherosclerotic plaque may include cholesterol, fats, calcium, bacteria, and platelets.

one of these clots travels to the heart and lodges in one of the coronary arteries that supply the heart muscle, a heart attack can occur. A clot that travels to the brain and lodges in a small vessel there will cut off the blood and oxygen supply to the area of the brain supplied by that vessel. This causes the neurons in that area to be injured or die from lack of oxygen. This type of stroke is called an **ischemic stroke**. (Ischemia is a lack of oxygen due to the loss of blood supply.) Extreme narrowing of the blood vessels that supply the brain can also result in ischemia. Hypertension can cause blood vessels in the brain to weaken over time and rupture, causing a **hemorrhagic stroke**.

Metabolic syndrome, also known as **syndrome X,** is a cluster of factors that tend to occur together and that have been associated with an increased risk of cardiovascular disease. These factors include hypertension, excessive abdominal fat (**central obesity**), insulin resistance, low HDL ("good" cholesterol) levels and high triglyceride (fatty acid) levels, high fibrinogen levels, and elevated blood levels of pro-inflammatory **C-reactive protein**. Research has shown that people who have metabolic syndrome are more likely to have coronary artery disease, stroke, or **type 2 diabetes**. Approximately 20% to 25% of adult Americans have metabolic syndrome.

Since epinephrine and cortisol raise blood glucose levels, and cortisol also raises levels of fatty acids in the blood, chronic high levels of these hormones result in insulin resistance and a buildup of fatty materials in the blood. Although the exact mechanism by which insulin resistance occurs has not been determined, it is known that cortisol also acts directly on insulin receptors to desensitize them. High levels of cortisol cause an increase in abdominal fat as well as deposition of fat in artery walls. Most people with insulin resistance also have central obesity.

STRESS AND THE DIGESTIVE SYSTEM

Stress affects how much people eat and what they eat, as well as storage and mobilization of nutrients. About two-thirds of people eat more when they are under stress, while the other one-third eats less. The reasons for this have not yet been determined, but the type of stress, the pattern of stressors, the reactivity of the glucocorticoid system, and even attitudes toward eating may play a part. Along with the increase in appetite that often accompanies stress, people have a preference for carbohydrates during stress. During the recovery period after a stressor, glucocorticoids stimulate fat cells in the abdominal area to store fat.

Digestive processes slow down during stress. Saliva and digestive enzymes and acids are not secreted, and muscle contractions of the stomach and small intestine stop. Blood flow is shunted to the brain and to exercising muscles and away from nonexercising muscles and the digestive system. Contractions of the large intestine are increased by the sympathetic nervous system, and diarrhea may result.

Some diseases of the gastrointestinal tract are related to stress. There appears to be a link between stress and irritable bowel syndrome, which is characterized by diarrhea or constipation, abdominal pain and distention, and passage of mucus. The risk of irritable bowel syndrome is associated with chronic major stressors, which also make existing cases worse.

Just like Selye's rats, people can develop "stress ulcers" rapidly when subjected to intense stress for a number of days. Ulcers that develop gradually were once thought to be caused by stress. It turns out, however, that the root cause of these ulcers is an acid-resistant bacterium called *Heliobacter pylori* that lives in most people's stomachs. An overgrowth of this bacterium apparently occurs due to a combination of stress and lifestyle risk factors, such as smoking, alcohol use, skipping meals, and taking too many nonsteroidal anti-inflammatory drugs (NSAIDs). When other causes are factored out in a statistical analysis, stress causes the risk of ulcers to increase two to three times.

STRESS AND THE RESPIRATORY SYSTEM

Emotional arousal and stress have long been recognized to have an effect on respiration. Both cause an increase in the rate of respiration and a decrease in carbon dioxide levels in the blood. Conversely, breathing patterns have been shown to affect emotions. A slower breathing rate has been shown to reduce anxiety, whereas hyperventilation has the opposite effect.

There also appears to be a relationship between emotional stress and respiratory disorders such as **asthma**. Emotional factors, such as anxiety, laughter, anger, resentment, or humiliation, have been found to precipitate an asthma attack in a certain percentage of individuals. Precipitation of an asthma attack in some people has also been found to correlate with life events, such as bereavement, injury to relatives, illness, financial difficulties, marital conflicts, and problems at work.

Asthma is an inflammatory disease, in that the airways of a person with asthma are always inflamed. There are two phases to an asthma attack: an early phase, in which the muscles surrounding the airways constrict, and a late phase, in which the airways become more inflamed, producing swelling. Cells in the lining of the airways may also produce mucus. All of these symptoms have the net effect of reducing airflow through the airways.

A complex and not yet clearly understood interaction between hormones, immune factors, and the autonomic nervous system produces the symptoms of asthma. One study in children showed that those with asthma had lower levels of cortisol in the blood, particularly during the night. Cortisol normally curbs the inflammatory response, so lower levels of this hormone could be one of the contributing factors to this disease. Increases in blood levels of epinephrine and norepinephrine also cause an increase in the susceptibility of the airways to inflammation. Airway resistance therefore increases during emotional arousal and stress.

STRESS AND THE IMMUNE SYSTEM

The cells of the immune system are the white blood cells, or **leukocytes**. There are three basic types of leukocytes: lymphocytes, monocytes, and granulocytes. All blood cells develop from stem cells in the bone marrow. Red blood cells complete their maturation in the bone marrow before entering the bloodstream. Some white blood cells mature completely in the bone marrow, and others travel to finish maturation in the **thymus gland**. (Those that mature in the thymus gland are called **T lymphocytes**, or, for short, T cells.) After maturation, these immune cells pass from the bone marrow and thymus gland through the bloodstream to the lymph nodes and spleen. Some immune cells remain there and produce antibodies and **phagocytize**, or engulf and destroy, microorganisms that filter through the lymphatic system. Other immune cells leave the bloodstream to transit to sites of infection or tissue injury (Figure 7.2).

Cytokines, secreted by the leukocytes, are the **immunotransmitters**, or chemical messengers, of the immune system. Cytokine receptors are found on leukocytes, the lymphoid organs, and neurons. **Interleukin-1**, a cytokine produced during inflammatory reactions, can act on the hypothalamus as well as the pituitary gland to stimulate the release of corticotrophin-releasing hormone and ACTH, thereby activating the hypothalamic-pituitary-adrenal axis. This may be a feedback response to prevent the inflammatory response from spinning out of

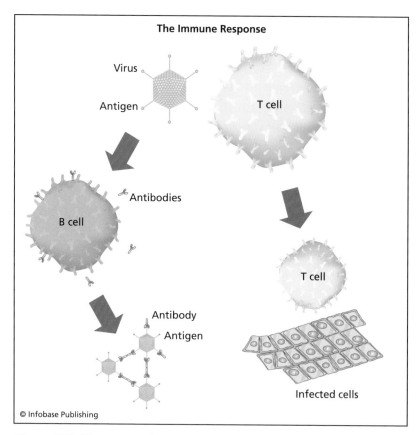

The Immune Response

Virus

Antigen

T cell

Antibodies

B cell

Antibody

Antigen

T cell

Infected cells

© Infobase Publishing

Figure 7.2 The two major types of lymphocytes are B lymphocytes (B cells for short) and T lymphocytes (T cells for short). When a virus (or other microorganism) invades the body, T helper cells stimulate a proliferation of T cells and B cells. B cells release antibodies that bind to the antigen (unique marker protein) on the surface of the virus. This either blocks the viruses from entering cells or causes them to clump together. Cytotoxic T cells release microscopic granules that contain chemicals that kill tumor cells and pathogen-infected cells.

control. Interleukin-1 is also the first alarm signal for the cascade of events known as the immune response when a microbial invader is detected.

Lymphoid organs (bone marrow, thymus gland, spleen, and lymph nodes) are all innervated by the autonomic nervous system. Both parasympathetic and sympathetic fibers synapse on these organs of the immune system. Neurotransmitter receptors for norepinephrine, epinephrine, dopamine, acetylcholine, serotonin, opioids, and GABA are found on leukocytes and on lymphoid organs. Glucocorticoid receptors are also present on leukocytes.

There is a lot of crosstalk between the immune system and the nervous system, as well as with the HPA axis. During stress, whether it is physical or psychological, and the subsequent recovery from stress, there is an intimate regulation of the various elements of the immune system by the sympathetic nervous system and cortisol. The cytokines in turn influence both the nervous system and the endocrine system.

In the first 30 minutes of the stress response, the combined action of the sympathetic nervous system and cortisol actually enhances the immune response. Cortisol stimulates cells of the immune system to leave the bloodstream and transit to the lymph nodes and skin. Discovered by Firdaus Dhabhar and Bruce McEwen, this process is known as **stress-induced trafficking**. This happens whether there is an actual threat of physical injury or whether the stressor is psychological, such as performing mental arithmetic in front of an audience. By one hour after the initiation of the stress response, the sustained activation of the sympathetic nervous system and the HPA axis begins to suppress the immune response and bring it back to baseline.

In the case of a major stressor that does not go away (chronic stress), the continued suppression of the immune system can cause the activity of the immune system to fall as much as 40% to 70% below the original baseline. Chronic stress, whether physical or psychological, will suppress the production of lymphocytes and their release into the bloodstream, the synthesis of **antibodies**, and the release of cytokines. By suppressing inflammation, stress inhibits the body's first line of defense against invading pathogens. Glucocorticoids can also kill lymphocytes, particularly T cells, by triggering programmed cell death, or **apoptosis**, in which cells essentially self-destruct. Suppression of immune function by cortisol has been studied more than that by the sympathetic nervous system, but there are studies that indicate that the sympathetic nervous system plays an important role in stress-induced immune suppression.

STRESS AND AUTOIMMUNE DISEASE

Suppression of the immune system by chronic stress can weaken the body's defenses against pathogens. One famous series

Type A Personality

In the 1950s, Ray Rosenman and Meyer Friedman introduced the theory that the type of personality one has may be related to one's risk of having heart disease. They labeled a set of personality characteristics that include constant striving, impatience, competitiveness, hostility, and urgency, as type A personality. The opposite, more easygoing type of personality they labeled type B personality. They found that men who were found to have a type A personality had twice the risk of developing cardiovascular disease within the 8 1/2 years before the next follow-up. S.A. Lyness reported in 1993 that the stress hormones, blood pressure, and heart rate of men with type A personalities were higher than those of type B when they were playing video games or subjected to criticism.

More recent research has found that only certain of the type A personality traits are actually related to risk of cardiovascular disease. Negative emotions such as hostility or chronic of studies conducted by Sheldon Cohen and his colleagues at Carnegie Mellon University showed that subjects exposed to a cold virus were three times more likely to catch a cold if they had recently experienced prolonged stress. Immune suppression can also set the body up for the development of autoimmune disease and inflammatory disorders such as allergies. With allergies, the immune system goes into overdrive in response to things like dust, pollen, or foods. **Autoimmune disease** develops when the immune system mistakes one of the body's own proteins for a foreign **antigen** and produces antibodies to it. This results in the destruction of the healthy tissue in which this protein is found.

anger do seem to predict a greater risk. In a recent 6-year prospective study, subjects who had a high anger score had 2.5 times the risk of sudden cardiac deaths or heart attacks during that period. Pessimism also seemed to be a risk factor. Laura Kubzansky and her coworkers found that over a 10-year prospective study the risk of developing heart disease was more than twice as great for pessimists than for optimists. Depressed adults were found to have an increased risk of heart disease in a 12-year prospective study conducted by researchers at the U.S. Centers for Disease Control and Prevention. On the brighter side, a group of Catholic nuns who expressed love, happiness, and positive feelings in brief autobiographies at age 22 lived 7 years longer on average than a group of Catholic nuns who expressed more negative emotions. By the time they were 80 years old, 24% of those who had expressed positive emotions had died, as compared to 54% of their counterparts.

More than 80 autoimmune diseases have been identified, including multiple sclerosis, rheumatoid arthritis, and **type 1 diabetes**. Multiple sclerosis destroys the **myelin sheath,** which surrounds and insulates nerve fibers. Cartilage is attacked in rheumatoid arthritis. The pancreas's islet cells, which produce insulin, are destroyed in type 1 diabetes. Stress makes these conditions worse, and evidence is accumulating to indicate that stress may play a role in their development.

■ **Learn more about the contents of this chapter** Search the Internet for *autoimmune disease, cytokine,* and *metabolic syndrome.*

8 | Stress and the Brain

Having finished his postdoctoral training, Bruce McEwen started working in the laboratory of behavioral neuroscientist Neal Miller in 1966. During this time, he and physiologist Jay Weiss collaborated on a series of studies in which they tried to locate receptors for corticosterone in the rat brain. To their surprise, the hippocampus was the brain structure that retained the most of an injection of radiolabeled corticosterone. McEwen soon had his own laboratory at Rockefeller University. By 1976, his research team had discovered the receptors for corticosterone in the hippocampus. Over the years, McEwen's laboratory has studied a broad range of stress-related topics, including the effects of stress on **neuroplasticity** and gene expression. A number of other famous stress researchers, including Robert Sapolsky, Elizabeth Gould, and Ron de Kloet, trained in McEwen's laboratory at Rockefeller University as students or postdoctoral fellows.

Robert Sapolsky was a graduate student in McEwen's research laboratory at Rockefeller University during the 1980s. While under McEwen's mentorship, Sapolsky mapped the locations of corticosterone receptors in the rat brain and studied the effects of stress on glucocorticoid receptor numbers and on neuronal survival in the rat hippocampus.

Together with McEwen and Lewis Krey, he came up with the glucocorticoid cascade hypothesis, which relates increasing levels of glucocorticoids to the aging process and disease. Sapolsky later established his own successful stress research laboratory at Stanford University. The research teams of these two outstanding neuroendocrinologists have made an enormous contribution to what we know about the impact of the stress response on the brain and on health in general.

STRESS AND THE HIPPOCAMPUS

Not only is the hippocampus the brain structure with the most glucocorticoid receptors, but it also helps regulate cortisol levels. There are two types of glucocorticoid receptors in the hippocampus, Type I and Type II. Cortisol is 10 times more likely to bind to **Type I glucocorticoid receptors**, and more than 90 % of these are occupied by cortisol at all times. It is during chronic stress or when cortisol levels are very high for other reasons that **Type II glucocorticoid receptors** are occupied.

Type II glucocorticoid receptors participate in the negative feedback response that regulates the levels of cortisol so that they do not get too high (Figure 8.1). In other words, the hippocampus helps shut off the activation of the HPA axis after stress. As the brain ages, this negative feedback mechanism does not work as well, and higher levels of circulating glucocorticoids are present. The higher levels of glucocorticoids in turn contribute to many of the diseases of old age.

McEwen's lab has discovered that chronic stress causes the dendritic branches of neurons in the hippocampus to shrink, or atrophy. **Dendritic remodeling** is the term they used to describe this process. Chronic stress also suppresses the formation of new cells in the **dentate gyrus.** This causes the hippocampus to become smaller. Monica Starkman and her research team at the University of Michigan found that in

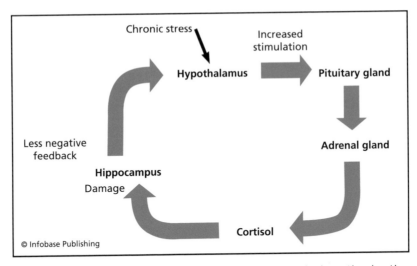

Figure 8.1 According to the glucocorticoid cascade hypothesis, the high levels of cortisol produced by chronic stress will eventually cause damage to the cells in the hippocampus, which helps regulate cortisol levels. This results in even higher levels of cortisol, which over time causes damage to tissues and organs and accelerates the process of aging.

patients with Cushing's disease, the hippocampus was smaller than in normal subjects and that this difference was proportional to cortisol levels.

The good news is that dendritic remodeling and the suppression of neurogenesis can be reversed if the levels of glucocorticoids are reduced soon enough. Starkman and coworkers used neuroimaging to look at the brains of Cushing's disease patients after their cortisol levels had been corrected. They found that the brains of these patients had begun to return to their normal size. Animal studies have yielded similar results. Bruce McEwen believes that this reduction in plasticity and neurogenesis during chronic stress is a protective measure.

There is a point of no return, however, in which cell death in the hippocampus can occur if high levels of glucocorticoids are sustained long enough. According to the glucocorticoid cascade hypothesis, repeated or chronic stress can accelerate or even cause the degeneration of the hippocampus that occurs with aging. In addition, the high levels of glucocorticoids that accompany neurological incidents, such as stroke, trauma, or seizures, can add to the toxicity of the incident. This is partly due to the fact that high levels of glucocorticoids for periods longer than about 30 minutes inhibit glucose availability to neurons by up to 25%. This reduction in the supply of glucose makes it harder for endangered neurons to survive.

STRESS AND MEMORY

Located in the temporal lobe adjacent to the lateral ventricle, the hippocampus is important for three types of memory: **episodic memory**, **semantic memory**, and **spatial memory** (Figure 8.2). Spatial memory helps us remember where things are located. Animals that store food in a lot of different places have large hippocampi. So do London taxi drivers, who must study the layout of London streets for two or more years and pass a difficult test before they can drive a taxi there.

Episodic memory is the type of memory we use for events, or episodes, in our lives. Semantic memory is where we store facts about which we hear or read. Episodic and semantic memory are two types of **declarative memory**, or **explicit memory**. Explicit memory is memory that can be accessed consciously and put into words, or "declared." **Implicit**, or **nondeclarative**, memory is another type of memory that is not available consciously. It includes **procedural memory**, or rule learning, and motor memory, or skill learning. **Classical conditioning** is another example of implicit memory. Pavlov's dogs salivating at the sound of a bell is probably the best known example of classical conditioning.

Damage to the hippocampus impairs the ability to learn new information. The most famous example of what happens after

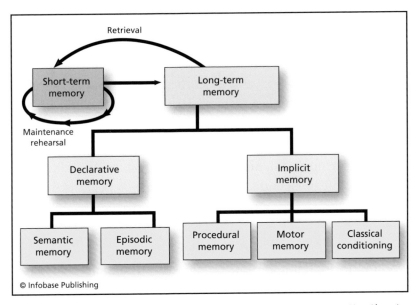

Figure 8.2 Information in the environment that one pays attention to can become part of short-term memory, especially if it is rehearsed. Some of this information is used for tasks at hand, such as dialing a phone number, and then is forgotten. More important or frequently used information may be stored in long-term memory. Declarative knowledge is available to conscious recall and includes factual (semantic) knowledge and memory of life events (episodic). Memories that are apparently stored in areas of the brain not accessible to conscious recall include memories of skills and rules.

hippocampal damage is the case of patient H.M. About two inches of H.M's temporal lobe was surgically removed on each side in 1953 in an attempt to correct epileptic seizures. Among the structures removed were about two-thirds of the hippocampus as well as the amygdala and the overlying cortex. After the surgery, H.M. could no longer form new declarative memories. His memory for past events and information is intact up until about 11 years before his surgery, which occurred at age 27. So as far as his memory of the world around him, H.M. was essentially frozen in time at age 16. H.M. can learn new motor skills, so his implicit memory is not affected. He cannot, however, remember having learned them. This would require forming a new episodic memory, which he can no longer do. Now in his eighties, H.M. has been able to learn a small amount of semantic information, such as the name of the president assassinated in 1963. This surprised the scientists who have been studying him for many years and is thought to indicate that there are multiple memory systems in the brain.

Formation of new declarative memories appears to involve neural pathways in the hippocampus that utilize the excitatory neurotransmitter glutamate. A process called **long-term potentiation** is induced at the synapses in these pathways, making them more excitable for longer periods. More than one type of glutamatergic receptor is involved in long-term potentiation. Typically, glutamate stimulates **AMPA receptors**, which open to allow sodium ions in to change the neuron's electrical properties to a point at which **NMDA receptors** open to allow calcium to enter the neuron. Calcium activates enzymes that cause many changes within the cell. Some of these changes may underlie the formation of new dendritic branches and synapses. Although the effects of the processes are not clearly understood yet, long-term potentiation and the formation of new synapses are involved in memory consolidation, the storage of new memories.

Acute stress actually facilitates memory consolidation. A lot of glucose is needed to provide energy for the neurons as they engage in memory processes. As we have learned, one of the jobs that norepinephrine, epinephrine, and cortisol perform is to increase the amount of glucose in the bloodstream during stress. The sympathetic nervous system also arouses the hippocampus to make it more alert and activated. Short-term stress even makes the receptors in the sense organs more sensitive.

Chronic stress, however, can cause memory problems. Cushing's disease patients, who have high levels of cortisol, have declarative memory problems. Declarative memory problems are also seen in patients undergoing prolonged treatment with synthetic glucocorticoids for inflammatory or autoimmune disorders. Even healthy volunteers given high doses of these compounds develop declarative memory problems after a few days. Patients who receive nonsteroidal anti-inflammatory compounds for inflammatory disorders do not develop these memory problems.

Since the formation of new synapses is important in memory consolidation, the shrinkage of dendritic branches in response to high glucocorticoid levels probably contributes to stress-related memory problems. Neurogenesis is decreased by just a few hours of high glucocorticoids or stress. So the decrease in neurogenesis may be another factor in the memory problems seen with high glucocorticoid levels.

STRESS AND POST-TRAUMATIC STRESS DISORDER

Neuroimaging techniques allow scientists to look at the brains of people who have undergone severe stress, such as combat stress or childhood abuse. **Post-traumatic stress disorder (PTSD)** is characterized by nightmares and flashbacks of the trauma and occurs in about 15% of individuals who have experienced severe trauma. In about half of PTSD patients, the hippocampus is smaller than usual and memory impairment is present.

STRESS AND DEPRESSION

Glucocorticoid levels have been shown to be high in about half of patients with major depression, a severe depressive state of more than two weeks in duration. It has been debated whether stress is a factor in the development of this disorder. Many of the changes in the neurotransmitter systems (norepinephrine, serotonin, dopamine) that have been implicated in depression can be caused by glucocorticoids. Glucocorticoids can alter the rate of synthesis of each of these neurotransmitters, the rate at which they are broken down, the number of their receptors, and the sensitivity of their receptors. In addition, the hippocampi of patients who have had long bouts of depression tend to be smaller than average. People with depression also tend to have impairments in declarative, or hippocampal-dependent, memory.

STRESS AND THE AMYGDALA

Collaborative studies between Bruce McEwen's team at Rockefeller University and Rupshi Mitra's team at the National Centre for Biological Sciences in Bangalore, India, have shown

Learned Helplessness

In the 1960s, Martin Seligman at the University of Pennsylvania was studying avoidance learning. In this type of learning, an animal can avoid a shock by performing a particular behavior after a warning stimulus occurs, or it can escape the shock by performing the behavior after the shock begins. In one such experiment, Seligman used two groups of dogs. A random series of mild electrical shocks was delivered to the feet of both groups of dogs. One group could either escape or avoid the shock by pushing a panel. For the other group, the shock was inescapable—they had no way of stopping it.

Next, Seligman tried to train the same two groups of dogs to jump over a hurdle to avoid shock in response to a warning light. The dogs that had experienced escapable shock had no problem learning the new task. The dogs that had experienced inescapable shock did not even try to escape the shocks by jumping over the hurdle. Many of these animals exhibited that stress has the opposite effect on plasticity in the amygdala. They have shown that **immobilization stress**, a model of psychological stress, causes an increase in the number of dendritic spines in the basolateral amygdala in rats. (In the immobilization stress model, the rat is confined in a clear plastic cylinder so that its movements are restricted but no physical discomfort or pain is experienced. Stress hormone levels increase in the rat's bloodstream when it is confined in this manner.)

STRESS AND ANXIETY

Anxiety-related symptoms also develop in rats after immobilization stress. This makes scientists wonder if stress contributes

symptoms, such as apathy and loss of appetite, that reminded Seligman of depression in humans.

Seligman and his colleagues conducted many more experiments on learned helplessness, the name he used to describe this phenomenon. Learned helplessness became an animal model for depression. Not all scientists agreed with his interpretation of the research results, so the model eventually fell into disuse.

There may yet be something interesting to learn from Seligman's experiments. It is now known that both stress and depression cause a decrease in neurogenesis in the hippocampus. Some scientists believe that neurogenesis may be necessary for some types of learning. If this is true, then it may be that learned helplessness was actually a failure to learn because of the physiological effect of stress on the hippocampus.

to the development of anxiety disorders. The stress hormones norepinephrine and epinephrine, rather than glucocorticoids, appear to be involved in the production of anxiety.

It has been speculated that since memory functions in the hippocampus are compromised while those of the amygdala are increased during stress, the context of fearful memories may be lost, leaving a free-floating type of anxiety. A particular stimulus may set off an alarm in the amygdala without the context from the hippocampus to explain its significance.

STRESS AND ADDICTION

Many things give us pleasure, such as good food, beautiful sights, and hard-won accomplishments. Anticipation of these natural rewards stimulates the release of dopamine into the nucleus accumbens from nerve endings projecting from the ventral tegmental area in the midbrain. This is the core of the reward pathway, also known as the pleasure pathway, which extends farther to include structures such as the amygdala and the prefrontal cortex. Stimulation of this pathway is one thing that natural rewards and addictive drugs have in common. The difference is that natural rewards increase the dopamine levels in this pathway by 50% to 100%, but addictive drugs increase it far above the normal level. For example, cocaine causes dopamine release to increase by one-thousandfold.

Stress causes a transient increase in dopamine levels, so if a stressor occurs just before drug exposure, it increases the addictive potential of a drug. Stress during development also increases the likelihood of becoming dependent on addictive drugs later in life. Maternal stress during pregnancy, birth complications, and stress during infancy have been shown to be associated with an increased potential for addiction in both rat and human studies. It is thought that stress during development may change the sensitivity of the dopaminergic pathways.

Not only does stress increase the risk of addiction, but it also makes withdrawal more painful. During withdrawal, brain corticotrophin-releasing hormone levels are increased tenfold, and glucocorticoids are elevated. (Corticotrophin-releasing hormone acts as a neurotransmitter in the brain and is thought to be involved in anxiety.) Relapse is also more likely to occur after stress, especially in an environment previously associated with drug use. Stressors that are uncontrollable or unpredictable have the greatest impact. Mild stressors, however, are often cited after relapse, leading some scientists to believe that addicts may be hypersensitive to stress.

■ Learn more about the contents of this chapter Search the Internet for *reward pathway*, *learned helplessness*, and *long-term potentiation*.

9 | Coping with Stress

Why do some people seemingly sail through life to age 100 and beyond and have little or none of the diseases that those 20 years their junior have? What is different about people who age successfully and those who die early of heart disease or stroke? Why are some people stressed out by the pressures of everyday life while others seem to have energy to spare? Is it in the genes, or are there some secrets that all of us should know about? Actually, there is a small genetic component, but there are a number of ways that have been found to counteract the effects of stress. Most of them are simply part of a healthy life-style that is often neglected in our everyday efforts to get more done in less time.

EXERCISE AND HEALTH

Regular moderate exercise has been shown to have many health benefits. These include a number of ways in which exercise helps us cope with stress. Many of the diseases that are caused by or worsened by stress are improved by exercise. Among these are diabetes, cardiovascular disease, and a suppressed immune system. Exercise is one of the ways that we can reduce our risk of stress-related illness.

EXERCISE AND DIABETES PREVENTION

One study conducted by the National Institutes of Health (NIH) involved participants who were at risk for type 2 diabetes because they had impaired glucose tolerance and were overweight. One group ate a low-fat diet and exercised 5 days a week for 30 minutes, with most of them choosing walking. The second group was given the diabetes medication metformin. In the group that exercised and consumed the low-fat diet, the risk of diabetes was reduced by 58%. In comparison, the risk of diabetes was reduced by only 31% in the group that took metformin. Exercise may have prevented or overcome insulin resistance by increasing the rate that glucose was taken up by muscle tissue.

Exercise and Cardiovascular Disease

Exercise also helps prevent or reverse cardiovascular disease. In one study, the risk of heart disease declined in proportion to the distance walked by a group of more than 2,500 elderly men. Aerobic exercise, such as walking, running, swimming, or biking, done on a regular basis reduces blood pressure and heart rate. Regular exercise reduces mortality from coronary artery disease and increases the blood supply to the heart muscle by improving the function of the lining, or endothelium, of the blood vessels that supply the heart. Exercise also causes the cardiac muscle cells to grow larger, resulting in a larger, stronger heart. This is in contrast to the effects of hypertension, which increase the size of the heart by stimulating **fibrosis**, or the formation of connective tissue, a process that weakens the heart. In the voluntary (active) musculature, exercise stimulates the formation of new capillaries (**angiogenesis**) and increases the diameter of some of the arteries (**arteriogenesis**). An interesting recent finding by M.J. Mayo and his colleagues in Singapore is that abdominal fat is lost preferentially during exercise—the exact opposite of stress-induced weight gain! This is an important factor in reducing metabolic syndrome symptoms that predispose a person to heart disease.

Exercise and the Immune System

Research on the effects of exercise on the immune system indicate that moderate exercise is immunoenhancing whereas intense exercise is immunodepressing. You will recall that acute stress enhances immune function whereas chronic stress depresses it. This may be partly due to their comparative effects on the stress response. In one study, people who engaged in moderate exercise in the form of near-daily brisk walking had half the number of sick days as controls over the next 12 to 15 weeks. Exercise more than 90 minutes in duration, however, may weaken the immune system for a period of 3 to 72 hours, during which time susceptibility to upper respiratory infections is increased.

Exercise and Tension Release

Now that we have seen how exercise can counteract the effects of stress over an extended period of time, we will look at the benefits we are likely to notice right away. One of these is the release of pent-up physical and emotional tension. With most stressors faced today, the fight-or-flight response prepares for but does not lead to increased motor activity. Exercise allows for a release of muscular tension. Muscle tension was shown in one study to decrease by more than 50% for as long as 90 minutes after bicycling, walking, or jogging. Mental relaxation is also one of the benefits of exercise. Rhythmic breathing, as well as the rhythmic movements of some forms of exercise, increases the number of **alpha waves** in the electroencephalogram. Alpha wave activity is characteristic of a relaxed state of mind.

Exercise and Mood

Exercise enhances mood and relieves anxiety and depression. Many people experience the euphoria that has become known as runner's high during exercise, with an enhanced mood for up to a day afterward. This is thought to occur as a result of the release during exercise of **endorphins** (natural opioids) as well as an increase in norepinephrine and serotonin levels. A 16-week study by Blumenthal and colleagues found that exercise was just as effective as the antidepressant Zoloft in reducing depression. A follow-up study found that the rate of relapse was significantly lower in the exercise group. In light of the extensive literature that demonstrates its beneficial effects, including reduction of depression and anxiety, Patrick Callaghan of City University London suggested that exercise remained a neglected intervention.

Exercise and Neurogenesis

It has been known for some time that exercise increases the rate of neurogenesis in the dentate gyrus of the hippocampus. In rats that are given free access to a running wheel, the rate of neurogenesis is more than twice as high as in control rats. Carl Ernst and his associates at the University of British Columbia have hypothesized that neurogenesis may be responsible for the reduction in depression seen with exercise. They further hypothesize that the increase in the levels of certain brain chemicals that occurs with exercise may be responsible for this increase in neurogenesis. For example, serotonin and B-endorphins, which increase during exercise, have been shown to cause an increase in neurogenesis. This is another way that exercise may help to stave off the effects of chronic stress, which has been shown to decrease neurogenesis.

NUTRITION

Like exercise, a nutritious diet is an important component of a healthy lifestyle, and it too has been shown to reduce the incidence of cardiovascular disease. Most scientists agree that a healthy diet should include plenty of whole grains and fresh fruits and vegetables with ample protein supplied by lean meats and fish. Excessive fat intake, refined sugar, and food additives should be avoided. Some fats, such as olive oil, flaxseed oil, and the body oils of cold water fish, have health benefits.

Given the depleted soils our food is grown in and the environmental toxins and stress that we are exposed to on a daily

Living to 100

Because of a reduction in the number of childhood deaths from infectious diseases, as well as better prevention and treatment of degenerative diseases, the average life expectancy in the United States is now 78 years, up from 46 years at the turn of the twentieth century. Centenarians (people who reach the age of 100 or more years), of whom 80% to 85% are women, are now the fastest growing segment of our population, with the 85+ age group coming in second. As the baby boomer generation ages, these groups will increase in size. About 1 in 10,000 Americans are 100 years old or more. In Nova Scotia, 1 in 5,000 people are centenarians. Okinawa, Japan, has the highest ratio of centenarians in the world at 50 per 10,000.

A number of large-scale studies have attempted to determine what factors contribute to the increased longevity of centenarians. Genetics is one of the first things that comes to mind. However, research studies have found that, while important, genetics accounts for less than one-third of the added longevity of centenarians. Most studies have found that a combination of factors appears to be responsible. These factors include strong basis, many people believe that nutrient supplements help maintain optimal health. Stress itself increases the body's use of vitamins, minerals, essential fatty acids, and essential amino acids. In addition to a good multivitamin supplement, those most commonly recommended are vitamins C, E, A, and D; the B vitamins; fish oil (containing **omega-3 fatty acids**); and minerals, particularly calcium. Vitamin D has received a lot of press recently because of studies indicating that it may protect against certain types of cancer.

social connections, excellent coping skills, zest for life, religious beliefs, emotional resilience, intellectual activity, appreciation of simple experiences and pleasures, self-sufficiency, a good sense of humor, low blood pressure, and not drinking heavily or smoking. Many centenarians play musical instruments. Women who have children after age 40 tend to be in better health and more likely to become centenarians.

An ongoing study of centenarians in Okinawa has found that a healthy lifestyle is an important factor in their longevity. Elderly Okinawans eat a diet that is high in fruits and vegetables, exercise regularly, avoid smoking, and consume alcohol little or not at all. They have a high intake of fiber, omega-3 and mono-saturated fatty acids, calcium in food and drinking water, and flavonoids (plant estrogens). Elderly Okinawans also have a tradition called hara hachi bu, whereby they eat only until they are 80% full. Optimism, social connectedness, and deep spirituality were also characteristic, especially among women. By observing many of the same factors that quench the effects of stress, these centenarians have lived to a predominantly healthy old age.

OMEGA-3 FATTY ACIDS

Research is showing, in general, that what is good for the heart is good for the brain. This is understandable, since a healthy cardiovascular system is necessary for the brain to get a constant supply of oxygen and glucose. For example, fish oils, which are rich in omega-3 fatty acids, have been shown to reduce the risk of heart attack and stroke. An increasing number of studies indicate that fish oils may also improve brain function. The adage that fish is brain food appears increasingly to be true. The reason for this appears to be that half of the brain's fat is made of **docosahexaenoic acid (DHA)**, a fatty acid that is also found in fish oil. Since 60% of the brain is made of fat found in cell membranes and in the myelin covering of axons, this is a pretty significant fact. DHA and **eicosapentaenoic acid (EPA)**, which is also found in fish oil, are long-chained omega-3 fatty acids. Some plant foods, such as walnuts, flaxseed, leafy greens, and avocados, contain short-chained omega-3 fatty acids, which can be converted to the long-chained variety by the body, although not very efficiently.

Psychopharmacologist Andrew Stoll gave a group of patients with **bipolar disorder** 10 grams of fish oil per day and found that after 4 months, 65% of these patients had greater reduction in symptoms than those given a placebo. (Formulas differ, but most fish oil contains about 180 mg of DHA and 120 mg of EPA per gram.) Just as striking was the relapse rate of 12% as compared to 52% with the placebo. (A placebo is a treatment that looks identical to the experimental treatment but does not have any physiological effect of its own.) Israeli scientist R.H. Belmaker and colleagues found that the depression scores of 7 out of 10 children in a group given omega-3 fatty acids were reduced by more than 50%, with remission occurring in 4 children. There is also evidence that fish oil may be beneficial for attention deficit/hyperactivity disorder (ADHD), as well as dyslexia.

British researcher Malcolm Peet found that schizophrenic patients had half the normal amount of DHA in their red blood cells, and that greater levels of deficiency were associated with more advanced symptoms. Peet and his coworkers saw a significant reduction in symptoms in a group of patients that were given 10 grams of a concentrated form of fish oil per day for a period of 6 weeks. Israeli researcher Shlomo Yehuda and his colleagues found an improvement of 74% in short-term memory and 58% in long-term memory in patients with Alzheimer's disease after one month of supplementation with a purified mixture of one part omega-3 to four parts omega-6 fatty acids. Scientists are also looking at fish oil as a potential treatment for alcoholism and drug abuse.

VITAMIN C

After the publication in 1970 of *Vitamin C and the Common Cold* by two-time Nobel Prize winner Linus Pauling, the American public increased its vitamin C intake by about 300%. There was subsequently a dramatic decrease in heart disease. This decrease occurred years before the first **statin** became available in 1987 and before aspirin use and diuretics became common treatment in the early 1990s.

Pauling and his colleague Matthias Rath conducted studies in guinea pigs in the 1990s that led them to develop new ideas about how heart disease develops. Guinea pigs, like humans, do not synthesize vitamin C from glucose like most vertebrates do. Like humans and unlike animals that synthesize vitamin C, guinea pigs develop atherosclerosis.

Pauling and Rath concluded that vitamin C deficiency causes the walls of blood vessels to weaken because of lowered **collagen** synthesis. (Vitamin C is a cofactor that is necessary for synthesis of the collagen protein.) Because of the lowered collagen content, stress fractures occur in blood vessels near points of mechanical stress, and a form of low-density lipoprotein called **lipoprotein A**, which has lysine receptors, adheres to lysine molecules in the broken strands of collagen. Because these receptors make lipoprotein A molecules "sticky," the atherosclerotic plaque continues to build. Pauling and Rath found that guinea pigs that had low blood levels of vitamin C also had high levels of lipoprotein A.

In another study, supplementation with more than 700 mg of vitamin C per day reduced the risk of death from heart disease by 62% of that associated with an intake of 60 mg per day (the recommended daily allowance) or less. Adhesion of white blood cells to the lining of blood vessel walls was reduced by supplementation with 2 grams of vitamin C per day. Numerous other studies have shown the benefit of vitamin C supplementation in reducing the risk of Alzheimer's disease, stroke, cataracts, cardiovascular disease, and cancer. In addition, asthma symptoms have been found to be reduced by 1 to 2 grams of vitamin C per day.

Based on the rate at which animals synthesize vitamin C, Pauling recommended an intake of 3 to 10 grams of vitamin C daily for optimal health. Varying estimates of minimal intake needed to avoid deficiency-related diseases have been made. Current thought is that a minimum intake of 200 mg per day, the amount found in 5 servings of fresh fruits and vegetables, is necessary to avoid a subclinical deficiency and the associated health problems. In cases of illness or advanced disease, much more may be necessary to regain health. Since vitamin C is eliminated so quickly (half within 30 minutes), 3 or 4 smaller doses about 4 hours apart are more effective than one large dose per day.

Individual requirements for vitamin C vary, so one individual may require more vitamin C than another. Biochemist Roger J. Williams and his colleague Gary Deason found that in guinea pigs, there was a twentyfold variation in vitamin C require-ments. Although vitamin C is considered virtually nontoxic, too much (this quantity varies with individuals) can cause diarrhea, irritability, or insomnia. These symptoms are easily corrected by reducing the dose.

Now we know that vitamin C prevents some of the same diseases that are worsened or contributed to by stress. Is there, however, a relationship between vitamin C and stress? Not unexpectedly, the answer to that question is yes. Many kinds of stress, including marathon running, infections, surgery, heart attack, stroke, head trauma, emotional stress, and even heat stress, reduce vitamin C levels in the blood. One reason for this may be that vitamin C is an important antioxidant that mops up free radicals generated during these events.

Vitamin C also has an intimate relationship with cortisol that is not yet completely understood. For example, the diurnal rhythms of vitamin C and cortisol are opposite, with the lowest levels of vitamin C occurring when cortisol levels are the highest. Interestingly, the highest levels of vitamin C in the human brain are found in the hippocampus, hypothalamus, and amygdala. Like the brain, the pituitary gland, ovaries, testes, leukocytes, adrenal cortex, and adrenal medulla contain high concentrations of vitamin C.

Although it is well known that vitamin C is essential as a cofactor in the production of epinephrine and norepinephrine, vitamin C's exact relationship with cortisol has not yet been determined. It is known that after ACTH stimulation, vitamin C is released from a rat adrenal gland before cortisol, reaches a peak, and then declines back to pre-ACTH levels while cortisol continues to rise. Stress or ACTH administration will deplete adrenal vitamin C.

Given in high doses, vitamin C appears to have a brak-ing action on the stress response. Samuel Campbell and his coworkers subjected rats to immobilization stress daily for one hour for three weeks. Stress hormone levels in rats that were fed 200 mg of vitamin C per day (equivalent to several grams for humans) were lower than those of controls. In addition, there was a reduction in the changes in the adrenal gland, spleen, and thymus as first described by Selye, as well as an increase in immunoglobulin G (IgG) antibody. (IgG antibodies are the most abundant antibodies and the most important for fighting viral and bacterial systemic infections.)

Surat Komindr and colleagues in Thailand found that in human adult males taking 4 grams of vitamin C per day, plasma cortisol levels were lower than those of controls. This occurred without affecting the diurnal rhythm of cortisol. In the same study, the plasma cortisol response to a small injection of ACTH was blunted. Researchers in Greece found that school-age children given 3 grams of vitamin C per day had significantly lower plasma cortisol after ACTH administration but no change in fasting cortisol levels prior to ACTH treatment.

More recently, German researcher Stuart Brody and his team administered 3 one-gram doses of sustained release vitamin C per day over a 14-day period to healthy young adults. Each day the research subjects were given a psychological stress test, which included mental arithmetic and public speaking. Both systolic and diastolic blood pressure and reports of anxiety were significantly lower in the group taking vitamin C for up to 40 minutes after the test.

SOCIAL SUPPORT

Many studies have shown the importance of a strong social network for withstanding the effects of stress. James S. House and his coworkers at the University of Michigan found that **social support** has a positive impact on health that is as significant as the negative impact of risk factors such as high blood pressure, smoking, or lack of exercise. Sheldon Cohen has found that the diversity of one's social network is more important than the number of people in determining susceptibility to the cold virus. Subjects with six types of social relationships (such as family, friends, neighbors, work associates, and social or religious groups) were one-quarter as likely to succumb to a cold as those with one to three types. The quality of a relationship is also important. Married couples who interact in a hostile manner have been found to have depressed immune systems.

RELIGION

Daniel Hall, who is both a physician and an Episcopal priest, recently performed a **meta-analysis** in which he combined and analyzed the results of a number of previous studies on longevity. He found that people who attend church regularly live 3.1 years longer, on average. This is roughly equivalent to the increase in lifespan found with regular exercise and cholesterol-lowering drugs.

Numerous other studies over the years have found a positive correlation between regular church attendance and improved health and longevity. Harold Koenig was in charge of a study at Duke University Medical Center involving 1,700 elderly subjects. In this study, it was found that religious observance was associated with enhanced immune function and lower blood pressure. Other health factors that have been found in other studies to be correlated with religious involvement include lower rates of hypertension, carotid atherosclerosis, and coronary artery obstruction.

Obviously, most people attend religious services to practice their faith. Embodied in most religious practices, however, are positive attitudes and behaviors that are also conducive to good physical health. Among these are altruism, gratitude, forgiveness, purpose, and hope. In addition, high-risk behaviors are discouraged. Involvement in religious activities is also a source of social support. So in addition to the spiritual benefits obtained, health and longevity are improved.

AVOIDANCE OF UNHEALTHY AND RISKY BEHAVIORS

It almost goes without saying that unhealthy and risky behaviors are themselves stress inducers, either physically or psychologically. Smoking, for example, is responsible for 4 million deaths per year worldwide, a figure that is expected to climb soon to 10 million. A person who starts smoking as a teen and does not quit has a 50% chance of dying from smoking-related illnesses, such as emphysema, lung cancer, and heart disease. Smokers are more likely to experience chronic disabilities, depression, and divorce. Added to the health risks is the addictiveness of tobacco smoking. There is a 1 in 3 chance of becoming hooked after the first cigarette. Once dependent, a smoker has a very difficult time quitting. As few as 3% are able to quit for as long as 6 months.

Excessive intake of alcohol has devastating effects not only on one's health but also on social and work relationships. The stimulation felt after one or two drinks is actually a result of the activation of the hypothalamic-pituitary-adrenal axis as a protective response to alcohol as a stressor. Animals whose adrenal glands have been removed will die if given what would normally be a "harmless" dose of alcohol. Chronic abuse of alcohol blunts the response of the HPA axis to alcohol in about half of alcoholics tested. As we have learned, a sluggish HPA axis puts a person at risk for inflammatory and autoimmune disease, not to mention alcohol toxicity. Long-term alcohol abuse can raise the risk of cancer, pancreatitis, ulcers, and liver disease. Even short-term abuse can increase the risk of automobile accidents, violence, loss of employment, and strained relationships.

Addictive drugs, such as cocaine, heroin, amphetamines, and prescription narcotics, can wreak havoc in the lives of those who become dependent on them. In addition to the interactions between stress and susceptibility to addiction, substance abuse is a stressor in its own right. Like alcohol abuse, substance abuse can damage physical health as well as relationships and careers. Alcohol and other addictive drugs can damage the brain over time, affecting memory and other cognitive functions. Even more dangerous is the potential for death from overdose.

There are other behaviors that can cause stress and put our health at risk. Some of them are obvious: an unhealthy diet, risky sexual behaviors, not wearing a seat belt, chronic loss of sleep, and overeating that leads to obesity. Others are more subtle, such as long hours at work that cause us to neglect activities that can help reduce our stress. Stress management can be complex, but it is worth the effort in terms of a longer, healthier life. In the end, the time spent engaging in a healthy lifestyle pays off in a better quality of life and in more years in which to pursue our goals and our dreams.

■ **Learn more about the contents of this chapter** Search the Internet for *centenarian, stress management,* and *lipoprotein A.*

Glossary

Action potential Electrical signal that carries the neural message down the axon.

Acute Short or temporary in duration.

Addisonian crisis Life-threatening physical crisis caused by an insufficient cortisol response to a stressor.

Addison's disease A disease in which the body does not produce enough cortisol; also known as hypocortisolism.

Adenohypophysis The anterior portion of the pituitary gland, which is part of the endocrine system.

Adipose tissue A type of body tissue that contains stored fat.

Adrenal gland Small endocrine gland located on top of the kidney.

Adrenal cortex The outer wall of the adrenal gland, which secretes several hormones, including cortisol.

Adrenal medulla The inner portion of the adrenal gland, which secretes epinephrine and norepinephrine.

Adrenergic Related to the neurotransmitter norepinephrine.

Adrenocorticotrophic hormone (ACTH) Hormone produced by the pituitary gland that stimulates the production of cortisol by the adrenal cortex.

Agonists Drugs that mimic the effects of a neurotransmitter at its receptor.

Alpha waves Brain-wave activity that occurs when resting quietly.

AMPA receptors Glutamatergic receptors that are activated by the agonist alpha-amino-3-hydroxy-5-methyl-4-isoxazolepropionic acid (AMPA).

Amygdala Subcortical nucleus located just in front of the hippocampus. Important in emotional regulation and the stress response.

Analog Structurally similar chemical compound.

Angiogenesis Growth of new capillaries.

Antagonists Drugs that block a neurotransmitter receptor and prevent the neurotransmitter from exerting its effects.

Antibodies Large Y-shaped proteins that have receptors at their tips to which a specific antigen binds; immunoglobulin.

Antigen A protein on the surface of a protein foreign to the body that is unique to that particular organism.

Anterior In the brain, toward the face.

Apoptosis Programmed cell death in which cells self-destruct.

Arteriogenesis Widening of existing arteries.

Association cortices (singular: cortex) Areas of the cerebral cortex that are involved in higher processing of information.

Asthma Inflammatory disorder that causes a restriction of airflow through air passages.

Atherosclerosis Accumulation of plaque that occurs at the site of an injury to a blood vessel that causes the central cavity of arteries to narrow; also referred to as "hardening of the arteries."

Autoimmune disease Disease in which the immune system mistakes one of the body's own proteins for an antigen and produces antibodies to it, resulting in the destruction of normal tissue.

Automaticity Automatic processing of a learned task so that it is done effortlessly without conscious thought about the steps in the process.

Autonomic nervous system Division of the peripheral nervous system that controls the muscle movements of the internal organs and glands.

Avoidance learning A type of fear conditioning in which a person or animal learns to avoid an aversive consequence, such as an electrical shock, after a warning stimulus comes on.

Axons Neuronal extensions that carry the neural message away from the neuron.

Axon terminal The area at the end of an axon from which neurotransmitter is released into the synaptic space.

Basal ganglia Nuclei located at the base of each cerebral hemisphere that are involved in the control of movement.

Basolateral nucleus Group of nuclei located laterally and at the base of the amygdala; the primary input nucleus for the amygdala.

Bipolar disorder A condition sometimes called manic-depressive disorder because periods of depression cycle with periods of mania (an excessively elevated mood).

Body language Nonverbal communication through facial expressions, body movements, and gestures.

Brain lateralization The establishment of one side of the brain as dominant for a particular function.

Brain stem The part of the brain that starts where the spinal cord leaves off and ends just below the diencephalon.

Central fissure The deep groove that runs longitudinally midway in the brain between the cerebral hemispheres.

Central nervous system The brain and spinal cord.

Central nucleus Group of nuclei in the amygdala that serves as the main output source from the amygdala.

Central obesity Fat accumulation in the abdominal area.

Central sulcus The horizontal groove across the surface of the brain approximately midway between the front and back of the brain.

Cerebellum Brain structure that forms the roof of the fourth ventricle; involved in motor coordination and the control of movements.

Cerebral aqueduct Narrow duct between the third and fourth ventricles of the brain.

Cerebral cortex The thin layer of nervous tissue that covers the cerebral hemispheres.

Cerebral hemispheres The two halves of the cerebrum, the largest part of the brain.

Cerebral ventricles Fluid-filled cavities in the brain.

Cerebrospinal fluid Fluid that fills and circulates through the cerebral ventricles and spinal canal and around the outside of the brain and spinal cord.

Chronic Long in duration; does not go away.

Cingulate gyrus Area of the cerebral cortex found on the medial surface of the brain and arching over the corpus callosum in midsagittal section.

Circadian rhythms Rhythms that fluctuate in a predictable manner over a 24-hour period.

Classical conditioning Type of learning in which a neutral stimulus that occurs just before a stimulus that produces a natural reflex comes to elicit the same reflex in the absence of the other stimulus.

Collagen Structural protein found in many body tissues, including muscle, skin, bone, and cartilage.

Commissures Large bundles of axons that connect structures on the two sides of the brain.

Conditioned emotional response Fear response, usually a cessation of activity, to a warning stimulus that predicts an aversive stimulus such as a footshock.

Conditioned fear Fear that has been conditioned to a particular stimulus; thought to be the source of human phobias.

Consolidation The process by which information is stored in long-term memory.

Context The environment, or surroundings, in which a stimulus or event occurs.

Contextual fear conditioning Fear conditioning to the context surrounding a stimulus or event.

Corpus callosum The largest of the cerebral commissures; a broad band of nerve fibers that connects the two cerebral hemispheres.

Corticotrophin-releasing hormone Hormone secreted by the paraventricular nucleus of the hypothalamus that travels in the hypophyseal portal system to the pituitary gland and stimulates the release of adrenocorticotrophin hormone (ACTH).

Cortisol Glucocorticoid hormone produced by the adrenal cortex in response to stimulation of the adrenal cortex by ACTH.

C-reactive protein A protein produced by the liver and found in plasma during acute inflammation; high levels of CRP are thought to be a risk factor for cardiovascular disease.

Cushing's syndrome Disorder in which too much cortisol is present in the body, caused by hypersecretion by a tumor or by the prolonged use of synthetic glucocorticoids; also called hypercortisolism.

Cytokines Chemical messengers of the immune system secreted by leukocytes.

Declarative memory Memory of events and information that is available for conscious recall.

Dendrites Extensions of a neuron that receive nerve signals from other neurons; usually shorter than an axon and on the opposite side of the cell body.

Dendritic remodeling Changes in the length and number of dendrites in response to hormones or other influences, such as exercise, learning, stress, or drugs.

Dendritic spines Tiny thornlike protruberances on a dendrite; provide extra surface area for synapses to occur.

Dendritic tree Term used to describe the many branchings of the dendrites of a neuron.

Dentate gyrus Structure in the hippocampal formation that receives input from the entorhinal cortex and passes it on to other hippocampal structures.

Diencephalon The area of the brain between the brain stem and the cerebrum; contains the thalamus and hypothalamus as well as the third ventricle.

Diurnal rhythm Rhythm that fluctuates over a 24-hour period and is synchronized with the light/dark cycle; a type of circadian rhythm.

Docosahexaenoic acid (DHA) Omega-3 fatty acid found in fish body oils and in some plant foods.

Dorsal prefrontal cortex Area of the cortex just above and before the cortex folds underneath the brain.

Duchenne smile A natural smile that includes the contraction of the orbicularis oculi muscles around the eyes as well as the zygomaticus major muscles of the cheeks.

Dysautonomia Dysregulation of the autonomic nervous system.

Ectopic ACTH syndrome Overproduction of ACTH due to an ACTH-producing tumor outside the pituitary.

Eicosapentaenoic acid (EPA) Long-chained omega-3 fatty acid found in fish body oils.

Electroencephalogram (EEG) A series of wavelike forms that describe the activity of an area of the brain over time.

Emotional blunting Inability to feel a normal level of emotions.

Emotional intelligence Ability to perceive, understand, and manage or regulate one's own emotions and those of others.

Emotional learning Learning of information that contains an emotional component.

Emotional memories Memories of information that contain an emotional component.

Emotional recognition Recognition of someone's emotion by their facial expressions or other behaviors.

Endorphins Natural opioids, or analgesics, released during exercise and stress.

Ependymal layer Layer of cells lining the lateral ventricles of the brain.

Episodic memory Memory of events in one's life.

Explicit memory Memory of factual information and events in one's life.

Facial feedback hypothesis Hypothesis that contracting the appropriate facial muscles for a particular emotion will trigger the physiological response for that emotion.

Fibrinogen Protein in the blood that causes platelets to be more likely to stick together and promotes clotting.

Fibrosis The pathological formation of connective tissue.

Fissure A groove on the surface of the brain that is deeper than a sulcus.

Flashbulb memories Vivid memories of where one was and what one was doing when one became aware of a historically significant event.

Frontal lobe The lobe of the cerebral hemisphere in the front of the brain in front of the central sulcus.

Functional magnetic resonance imaging (fMRI) A special type of MRI that can detect activity in the brain by detecting changes in blood oxygenation in areas of the brain involved in an activity.

General adaptation syndrome Set of symptoms that appears after chronic severe stress, including enlargement of the adrenal glands and shrinking of the spleen, thymus, and lymph nodes.

Glucocorticoid A steroid hormone produced by the adrenal cortex in response to ACTH; the primary glucocorticoid in humans is cortisol.

Granule cells Small neurons found in the dentate gyrus of the hippocampus as well as other areas of the brain.

Gray matter Nervous tissue composed primarily of neuronal cell bodies.

Gyri (singular: gyrus) Folds of cerebral cortex between sulci.

Hara hachi bu Tradition of Okinawan centenarians whereby they stop eating after they are 80% full.

Hemorrhagic stroke A stroke resulting from the rupture of a blood vessel.

Higher cognitive emotions Emotions that involve more conscious thought and are slower to develop than the basic emotions.

Hippocampus Limbic system structure involved in emotions and learning and memory.

Homeostasis Equilibrium or balance of the internal environment.

Hypercortisolism Excessive levels of cortisol caused by Cushing's disease or prolonged use of synthetic glucocorticoids.

Hyperphagia Overeating that leads to obesity.

Hypertension High blood pressure.

Hypocortisolism Abnormally low levels of cortisol.

Hypophyseal portal vessels Small veins and venules into which the capillaries of the median eminence empty, and which travel through the infundibulum and empty into capillaries in the anterior pituitary.

Hypothalamic-pituitary-adrenal (HPA) axis The hormonal pathway from the hypothalamus to the pituitary to the adrenal cortex.

Hypothalamus Brain structure located beneath the thalamus; functions include secretion of neurohormones that control the secretion of pituitary hormones; also triggers stress response by activating sympathetic nervous system and hypothalamic-pituitary-adrenal axis.

Immobilization stress An animal model of psychological stress; for example, rats are placed in clear plastic cylinders where their movement is restricted but no pain or discomfort is inflicted.

Immunotransmitters Chemicals produced by leukocytes to communicate with each other and with the nervous and endocrine systems.

Implicit memory Memory that is not readily available for conscious recall; includes classical conditioning and memory of skills and rules.

Infundibulum Stalk of the pituitary that attaches it to the hypothalamus.

Innate Inborn, unlearned.

Insula Floor of the lateral sulcus underneath the overlapping opercula (edges) of the frontal lobe and temporal lobe.

Insulin resistance Condition in which larger than normal amounts of insulin are needed to achieve the same effect as usual insulin levels.

Interleukin-1 Cytokine produced by macrophages during inflammatory reactions; first alarm signal of immune response.

Interneurons A neuron that acts as a relay between two other neurons.

Interpersonal space The space one maintains between himself and others.

Ischemic stroke Stroke caused by the blockage of a blood vessel due to a clot or to narrowing of the blood vessel.

Ketone bodies Chemicals produced by the liver during fatty acid metabolism; used by the brain as fuel in the absence of glucose during starvation.

Klüver-Bucy Syndrome Set of symptoms that results from bilateral removal of the anterior temporal lobe, which include emotional blunting, inability to recognize objects visually, and hyperphagia.

Lateral fissure Fissure that forms the upper boundary of the temporal lobe.

Lateral ventricle Ventricle found in the cerebral hemisphere on each side of the septum pellucidum.

Learned helplessness Condition that results from exposure to uncontrollable aversive stimuli and causes an individual to become unable to learn a new avoidance task.

Lesion studies Animal studies in which a brain structure is destroyed and behaviors are observed to determine what the function of the structure is.

Leukocytes White blood cells; the cells of the immune system.

Limbic system Group of brain structures involved in the regulation of emotions.

Lipoprotein A Type of low-density lipoprotein (LDL) that causes platelets to be more likely to stick together and promotes clotting.

Locus coeruleus Brain stem structure that produces norepinephrine and that has widespread projections to all areas of the brain.

Long-term potentiation Process by which rapid and repeated stimulation of a neural pathway results in an increase in excitability.

Lung surfactant A substance that reduces the surface tension of liquids coating the surfaces of the lungs so that air is absorbed more easily.

Macroelectrode In animal studies, unsharpened wires lowered into the brain for recording electrical activity. In humans, metal disks attached to the scalp with paste are used to record neural activity.

Magnetic resonance imaging (MRI) Neuroimaging technique that uses a magnetic field and radio waves to generate images of various sections of the brain.

Median eminence Small protuberance at the base of the hypothalamus to which the infundibulum of the pituitary is attached.

Meta-analysis A statistical technique in which the results from a number of studies are combined and analyzed.

Metabolic syndrome A group of risk factors that tend to occur together and are predictive of cardiovascular disease.

Microelectrode A very thin electrode that can be lowered into the brain for electrical recording without damaging the tissues.

Midsagittal A vertical section through the brain between the cerebral hemispheres.

Myelin sheath Fatty sheath around the axons of neurons that provides insulation and speeds the electrical signal.

Neural crest Group of cells that separates from the neural tube during embryonic development to become the peripheral nervous system.

Neurasthenia A nineteenth-century counterpart of chronic fatigue syndrome; known as nervous exhaustion.

Neuroendocrinology The study of the interplay of the nervous system and the endocrine system.

Neurogenesis The birth of new neurons.

Neurohormones Hormones secreted by a neuron.

Neurohypophysis The posterior portion of the hypothalamus, which is technically part of the brain because of its embryonic origin.

Neuroimaging techniques Noninvasive techniques to study the brain's interior; include PET scans and MRI scans.

Neuroplasticity The ability of the brain to reorganize and restructure to facilitate learning or recovery from injury or disease.

Neuroscience Study of the brain and nervous system.

Neurotransmitters Chemicals produced by brain cells that carry the neural message across the synapse.

Neurotransmitter receptor Receptor to which a particular neurotransmitter binds.

NMDA receptors Type of glutamatergic receptors that are thought to be involved in learning and memory.

Nondeclarative memory Memory that is not readily available for conscious recall; explicit memory.

Nucleotide A building block for DNA.

Nucleus (plural: nuclei) A group of neurons of similar function.

Nucleus accumbens Nucleus located ventral to where the caudate and the putamen come together near the lateral ventricle; it is an important structure in the reward pathway and is considered the interface between the limbic and motor systems.

Occipital lobe Area of cerebral cortex surrounding the pole (back part) of the brain and bounded in front by the parietal (above) and temporal (below) lobes. Contains the primary and secondary visual cortices.

Omega-3 fatty acids Long-chained fatty acids found in fish body oils and some plant foods.

Opercula (singular: operculum) Overlapping edges of either the frontal lobe or the temporal lobe overlying the insula at the lateral fissure.

Orbitofrontal cortex Area of cerebral cortex that overlies the bony orbits in which the eyes are found on each side.

Organelles Tiny structures within a cell that perform the life functions of the cell.

Oscilloscope Electronic device that allows electrical voltages to be viewed on a screen as a graph.

Parietal lobe Lobe of the brain located between the occipital lobe and the central sulcus and extending down to the lateral fissure.

Parasympathetic nervous system Division of the autonomic nervous system that maintains normal function in the body and returns the body to normal function after sympathetic activation.

Paraventricular nucleus Hypothalamic nucleus that produces oxytocin, vasopressin, corticotrophin releasing hormone and thyroid releasing hormone.

Periaqueductal gray Area of gray matter surrounding the cerebral aqueduct; involved in analgesia and behavioral activation.

Peripheral nervous system All components of the nervous system outside of the brain and spinal cord.

Phagocytize To consume by engulfing.

Phobia Irrational fear of particular objects, activities, or situations.

Physiological Relating to the healthy or normal functioning of an organism.

Pituitary gland The structure suspended beneath the hypothalamus; anterior portion is an endocrine gland, and posterior portion is neural tissue.

Placebo A treatment that is identical to an experimental treatment except that it has no physiological effect.

Plexi (singular: plexus) Networks of neurons and their processes.

Polygraph A device that measures heart rate, blood pressure, skin conductivity, and respiration while a person answers questions; commonly known as a lie detector.

Polymodal cortex Association cortex that integrates information from more than one of the senses.

Positron emission tomography (PET) scan A neuroimaging technique that can be used to measure metabolic rate of brain structures or concentrations of radiolabeled precursor molecules in particular brain structures.

Posterior In the brain, toward the back of the head.

Postganglionic neurons Peripheral neurons on which preganglionic neurons synapse.

Post-traumatic stress disorder (PTSD) Stress-related disorder caused by trauma or abuse; symptoms include flashbacks and nightmares.

Prefrontal cortex The part of the frontal lobe that lies in front of the motor and premotor areas and extends to the underside of the brain.

Prefrontal lobotomy Surgical technique in which the pathways that connect the prefrontal cortex with other areas of the brain are cut.

Preganglionic neurons Neurons in the brain stem and spinal cord that project to postganglionic neurons in the peripheral nervous system.

Primary adrenal insufficiency Condition in which too little cortisol is produced because of a problem at the level of the adrenal gland.

Primary sensory cortex (plural: cortices) Area of cortex that receives and processes sensory data relayed by the thalamus, with the exception that olfactory information goes to primary olfactory cortex before going to the thalamus.

Procedural memory Memory of skills or rules.

Psychic blindness Inability to identify an object visually; a symptom of Klüver-Bucy syndrome.

Radioactive tracer A molecule to which a radioactive isotope has been attached.

Receptors Special proteins to which neurotransmitters attach to produce their actions.

Secondary adrenal insufficiency Production of too little ACTH by the pituitary gland.

Secondary rewards Conditioned stimuli that have been repeatedly paired with natural rewards so that they cause the release of dopamine and the activation of the nucleus accumbens.

Selective attention Focusing on specific environmental stimuli and ignoring others.

Semantic memory Memory of facts and information.

Septal nuclei Subcortical nuclei located above the hypothalamus and just below the septum pellucidum in the area of the optic chiasm; sometimes included in the limbic system.

Septum pellucidum Thin membrane that separates the lateral ventricles.

Social support Network of friends, family, and acquaintances that provides emotional support in a variety of ways.

Soma Cell body of a neuron.

Somatic nervous system Subdivisions of the peripheral nervous system that carries sensory information from the sense organs to the central nervous system and carries motor commands from the central nervous system.

Spatial memory Memory of where things are located.

Statin Cholesterol-lowering drug.

Stimulus A detectable change in some aspect of the environment.

Stress-induced trafficking Movement of leukocytes to the lymph nodes and skin when stimulated by cortisol.

Stressors Environmental factors that the brain perceives to be some type of threat.

Subcortical nuclei Groups of neurons located in the cerebral hemispheres deep beneath the cortex.

Subependymal layer Layer of cells beneath the lining of the lateral ventricle that can differentiate into neurons.

Subgranular layer Layer of cells beneath the granular layer of the dentate gyrus that can differentiate into new neurons.

Sulcus A shallow groove between gyri on the surface of the brain.

Sympathetic nervous system Division of the autonomic nervous system that is responsible for the fight-or-flight response.

Synapse Tiny gap between nerve endings across which neurotransmitters diffuse to carry the neural signal.

Syndrome X A group of risk factors for cardiovascular disease that tend to occur together; also known as metabolic syndrome.

Temporal lobe Lobe of the cerebral cortex that extends forward from the occipital lobe and downward from the lateral sulcus.

Thymus gland Lymph organ located in the upper chest.

T lymphocytes Lymphocytes that mature in the thymus gland.

2-deoxyglucose (2-DG) Structural analog of glucose that cannot be metabolized by the cell and is therefore useful for neuroimaging studies when it is radiolabeled.

Type A personality Personality type that includes characteristics such as constant striving, impatience, competitiveness, hostility, and urgency.

Type B personality Easygoing personality type that lacks the distinguishing traits of the Type A personality.

Type 1 diabetes Juvenile onset diabetes; an autoimmune disease in which the islet cells of the pancreas that synthesize insulin are destroyed by the immune system.

Type 2 diabetes Adult onset diabetes; characterized by insulin resistance, in which larger than normal amounts of insulin are needed to achieve the same effect.

Type I glucocorticoid receptors High-affinity glucocorticoid receptors to which cortisol binds more readily; most of these receptors are occupied at all times.

Type II glucocorticoid receptors Low-affinity glucocorticoid receptors that are occupied only when cortisol levels are high; function to provide negative feedback on cortisol production.

Ventral medial prefrontal cortex Area of cortex found on the underside of the brain between the two orbitofrontal cortices.

Ventral tegmental area (VTA) Area in the midbrain that contains dopaminergic neurons that project to the nucleus accumbens and the prefrontal cortex.

Visual backward-masking Research technique in which a stimulus is presented briefly on a screen and is followed immediately by a second stimulus so that the subject has no conscious awareness of the first stimulus.

Vocal cues Changes in loudness, pitch, tempo, fluency, and inflection that signal emotional states.

Bibliography

Books and Journals

Aggleton, J.P., ed. *The Amygdala: A Functional Analysis*, 2nd ed. Oxford: Oxford University Press, 2000.

Babyak, M., J.A. Blumenthal, S. Herman, P. Khatri, M. Doraiswamy, K. Moore, W.E. Craighead, T.T. Baldewicz, and K.R. Krishnan. "Exercise Treatment for Major Depression: Maintenance of Therapeutic Benefit at 10 Months." *Psychosomatic Medicine* 62 (2000): 633–638. Available online. URL: *http://www.psychosomatic-medicine.org/cgi/reprint/62/5/633*. Accessed on December 19, 2006.

Berczi, Istvan, and Andor Szentivanyi. "The Immune-neuroendocrine Circuitry," in *NeuroImmune Biology Vol 3: The Immune-Neuroendocrine Circuitry: History and Progress.* Boston: Elsevier, 2003, 561–592.

Blanchard, C.R. Blanchard, J.M. Fellous, F.S. Guimarães, W. Irwin, J.E. LeDoux, J.L. McGaugh, J.B. Rosen, L.C. Schenberg, E. Volchan, and C. Da Cunha. "The Brain Decade in Debate: III. Neurobiology of Emotion." *Brazilian Journal of Medical and Biological Research* 34 (2001): 283–293.

Bloom, Floyd E., Charles A. Nelson, and Arlyne Lazerson. *Brain, Mind, and Behavior*, 3rd ed. New York: Worth Publishers, 2001.

Brody, S., R. Preut, K. Schommer, and T. H. Schurmeyer. "A Randomized Controlled Trial of High Dose Ascorbic Acid for Reduction of Blood Pressure, Cortisol, and Subjective Responses to Psychological Stress." *Psychopharmacology* (Berl) 159 (2002): 319–324.

Callaghan, P. "Exercise: A Neglected Intervention in Mental Health Care?" *Journal of Psychiatric and Mental Health Nursing* 11 (2004): 476–483.

Carlson, Neil R. *Physiology of Behavior*, 9th ed. Boston: Pearson Education, 2007.

Carper, Jean. *Your Miracle Brain*. New York: HarperCollins Publishers, 2000.

Carr, A. C., and B. Frei. "Toward a New Recommended Dietary Allowance for Vitamin C Based on Antioxidant and Health

Effects in Humans." *American Journal of Clinical Nutrition* 69 (1999): 1086–1107. Available online. URL: *http://www.ajcn.org/cgi/ reprint/69/6/1086.* Accessed on December 19, 2006.

Cleare, A. J. "The Neuroendocrinology of Chronic Fatigue Syndrome." *Endocrine Reviews* 24 (2003): 236–252. Available online. URL: *http:// edrv.endojournals.org/cgi/reprint/24/2/236.* Accessed on December 19, 2006.

Cooper, Cary L., and Philip Dewe. *Stress: A Brief History.* Malden, Mass.: Blackwell Publishing, 2004.

Davidson, Richard J., Klaus R. Scherer, and H. Hill Goldsmith, eds. *Handbook of Affective Sciences.* New York: Oxford University Press, 2003.

De Caterina, R., A. Zampolli, S. Del Turco, R. Madonna, and M. Massaro. "Nutritional Mechanisms that Influence Cardiovascular Disease." *American Journal of Clinical Nutrition* 83 (2006): 421S–426S.

Delarue, J., O. Matzinger, C. Binnert, P. Schneiter, R. Chioléro, and L. Tappy. "Fish Oil Prevents the Adrenal Activation Elicited by Mental Stress in Healthy Men." *Diabetes and Metabolism* 29 (2003): 289–295. Available online. URL: *http://www.masson.fr/masson/ portal/editorialproduct/ARTICLE.pdf?CodeRevue=DM&ProductCo de=535&PathXML=REVUE/DM/2003/29/3/ARTICLE1110832809. xml&path=REVUE/DM/2003/29/3/289/pdf_51347.pdf.* Accessed on December 19, 2006.

Dimberg, U., and L.O. Lundquist. "Gender Differences in Facial Reactions to Facial Expressions." *Biological Psychology* 30 (1990): 151–159.

Dolan, R. J., and P. Vuilleumier. "Amygdala Automaticity in Emotional Processing." *Annals New York Academy of Sciences* 1 (2003): 348–355.

Eriksson, P. S., E. Perfilieva, T. Bjork-Eriksson, A. M. Alborn, C. Nordborg, and D. A. Peterson. "Neurogenesis in the Adult Human Hippocampus." *Nature Medicine* 4 (1998): 1313–1317.

Ernst, C, A. K. Olson, J. P.J. Pinel, R. W. Lam, B. R. Christie, O. Ernst, C. J. Pinel. "Antidepressant Effects of Exercise: Evidence for an Adult-neurogenesis Hypothesis?" *Journal of Psychiatry and Neuroscience* 31:

(2006): 84–92. Available online. URL: *http://www.cma.ca/multimedia/staticContent/HTML/N0/l2/jpn/vol-31/issue-2/pdf/pg84.pdf.* Accessed on December 19, 2006.

Evans, Dylan. *Emotion.* New York: Oxford University Press, 2001.

Evans-Martin, F. Fay. *The Nervous System (Your Body: How It Works).* Philadelphia: Chelsea House Publishers, 2005.

Fischer, Agneta H, ed. *Gender and Emotion: Social Psychological Perspectives.* Cambridge: Cambridge University Press, 2000.

Gaab, J., D. Huster, R. Peisen, V. Engert, V. Heitz, T. Schad, T. H. Schurmeyer, and U. Ehlert. "Hypothalamic-Pituitary-Adrenal Axis Reactivity in Chronic Fatigue Syndrome and Health Under Psychological, Physiological, and Pharmacological Stimulation." *Psychosomatic Medicine* 64 (2002): 951–962. Available online. URL: *http://www.psychosomaticmedicine.org/cgi/reprint/64/6/951.* Accessed on December 19, 2006.

Gervais, D., M. D., and S. Saini, M. D. "Walter B. Cannon, MD." *Radiology* 194 (1995): 31–32. Available online. URL: *http://radiology.rsnajnls.org/cgi/reprint/194/1/31.pdf#search=%22Walter%20Cannon%20and%20peristaltic%22.* Accessed on December 19, 2006.

Gould, E., A. J. Reeves, M. Fallah, P. Tanapat, C.G. Gross, and E. Fuchs. "Hippocampal Neurogenesis in Adult Old World Primates." *Proceedings of the National Academy of Sciences* 27 (1999): 5263–5267.

Gould, E., P. Tanapat, B.S. McEwen, G. Flugge, and E. Fuchs. "Proliferation of Granule Cell Precursors in the Dentate Gyrus of Adult Monkeys is Diminished by Stress." *Proceedings of the National Academy of Sciences* 17 (1998): 3168–3171.

Gray, J. R., T.S. Braver, and M.E. Raichle. "Integration of Emotion and Cognition in the Lateral Prefrontal Cortex." *Proceedings of the National Academy of Sciences U. S. A.* 99 (2002): 4115–4120. Available online. URL: *http://www.pnas.org/cgi/reprint/99/6/4115.* Accessed on December 19, 2006.

Hairston, I. S., M.T. Little, M.D. Scanlon, M.T. Barakat, T.D. Palmer, R.M. Sapolsky, and H.C. Heller. "Sleep Restriction Suppresses

Neurogenesis Induced by Hippocampus-Dependent Learning." *Journal of Neurophysiology* 94 (2005): 4224–4233.

Herrington, J.D., A. Mohanty, N.S. Koven, J.E. Fisher, J.L. Stewart, M.T. Banich, A. G. Webb, G.A. Miller, and W. Heller. "Emotion-Modulated Performance and Activity in Left Dorsolateral Prefrontal Cortex." *Emotion* 5 (2005): 200–207.

Hubbard, John R., and Edward A. Workman, eds. *Handbook of Stress Medicine: An Organ System Approach.* Boca Raton, Fla.: CRC Press, 1998.

Hume, R., and E. Weyers, E. "Leukocyte Ascorbic Acid Levels After Acute Myocardial Infarction." *British Heart Journal* 34 (1972): 238–243.

Jacob, R.A., and G. Sotoudeh. "Vitamin C Function and Status in Chronic Disease." *Nutrition in Clinical Care* 5 (2002): 66–74.

Komindr, S., G. E. Nichoalds, and A. Kitabchi. "Bimodal Effects of Megadose Vitamin C on Adrenal Steroid Production in Man: An *In Vivo* Study." *Annals New York Academy of Sciences, 498* (1987): 487–490.

LeDoux, J.E. "Emotional Memory Systems in the Brain." *Behavioural Brain Research* 58 (1993): 69–79.

LeDoux, Joseph. *The Emotional Brain: The Mysterious Underpinnings of Emotional Life.* New York: Simon & Schuster, 1996.

Levinson, David, James J. Ponzetti, Jr., and Peter F. Jorgensen, eds. *Encyclopedia of Human Emotions* Vol 1. New York: MacMillan Reference USA, 1999.

———. *Encyclopedia of Human Emotions* Vol 2. New York: MacMillan Reference USA, 1999.

Liakakos, D., Douglas, N.L., Ikkos, D., Anoussakis, C., Vlachos, P. and G. Jouramani. "Inhibitory Effect of Ascorbic Acid (Vitamin C) on Cortisol Secretion Following Adrenal Stimulation in Children." *Clinica Chimica Acta* 65 (1975): 251–255.

Liggins, G. C. "The Role of Cortisol in Preparing the Fetus for Birth." *Reproduction, Fertility, and Development* 6 (1994): 141–150.

Linke, A., S. Erbs, and R. Hambrecht. "Exercise and the Coronary Circulation—Alterations and Adaptations in Coronary Artery Disease." *Progress in Cardiovascular Disease* 48 (2006): 270–284.

Matthews, Dale A., Michal E. McCullough, David B. Larson, Harold G. Koenig, James P. Swyers, and Mary Greenwold Milano. "Religious Commitment and Health Status: A Review of the Research and Implications for Family Medicine." *Archives of Family Medicine* 7 (1998): 118-124 Available online at *http:// archfami.ama-assn.org/cgi/content/full/7/2/118.*.

Mayo, M. J., J. R. Grantham, and G. Balasekaran. "Exercise-Induced Weight Loss Preferentially Reduces Abdominal Fat." *Medicine and Science in Sports and Exercise* 35 (2003): 207–213.

McEwen, Bruce S., and Elizabeth N. Lasley. *The End of Stress As We Know It.* Washington, D.C.: Joseph Henry Press, 2002.

McGaugh, J. L. "The Amygala Modulates the Consolidation of Memories of Emotionally Arousing Experiences." *Annual Review of Neuroscience* 27 (2004): 1–28.

Morris, C. G., and Albert A. Maisto. *Psychology: An Introduction*, 12th ed. Upper Saddle River, N.J,: Pearson Prentice Hall, 2005.

Myers, David G. *Psychology*, 7th ed. New York: Worth Publishers, 2003.

Nance, D. M., and B. J. MacNeil. "Immunoregulation by Innervation. The Immune-Neuroendocrine Circuitry," in *NeuroImmune Biology Vol 3: The Immune-Neuroendocrine Circuitry: History and Progress.* Boston: Elsevier, 2003.

Nemets, H., B. Nemets, A. Apter, Z. Bracha, and R.H. Belmaker. "Omega-3 Treatment of Childhood Depression: A Controlled, Double-Blind Pilot Study." *American Journal of Psychiatry* 163 (2006): 1098–1100.

Oatley, Keith. *Emotions: A Brief History.* Malden, Mass.: Blackwell Publishing, 2004.

Patak, P., H.S. Willenberg, and S.R. Bornstein. "Vitamin C Is an Important Cofactor for Both Adrenal Cortex and Adrenal Medulla." *Endocrine Research* 30 (2005): 871–875.

Pinel, John P.J. *Biopsychology*, 6th ed. Boston: Pearson Education, Inc., 2006.

Prior, B.M., P.G. Lloyd, H.T. Yang, and R.L. Terjung. "Exercise-Induced Vascular Remodeling." *Exercise and Sports Science Reviews* 31 (2003): 26–33.

Riad, M., M. Mogos, D. Thangathurai, and P.D. Lumb. "Steroids." *Current Opinion in Critical Care* 8 (2002): 281–284.

Roitt, Ivan M., Jonathan Brostoff, and David Male. *Immunology*, 5th ed. Philadelphia: Mosby, 1998.

Rupshi, M., J. Shantanu, B. S. McEwen, A. V., and S. Chattarji. "Stress Duration Modulates the Spatiotemporal Patterns of Spine Formation in the Basolateral Amygdala." *Proceedings of the National Academy of Sciences* 102 (2005): 9371–9376.

Sapolsky, Robert M. *Why Zebras Don't Get Ulcers*, 3rd ed. New York: Henry Holt and Company, 2004.

Schorah, C. J. "Vitamin C Status in Population Groups," in *Vitamin C (Ascorbic Acid)*. London: Applied Science, 1981, 23–47.

Song, Cai, Brian E. Leonard, and Brian Leonard. *Fundamentals of Psychoneuroimmunology*. New York: John Wiley & Sons, 2000.

Taylor, J. G., and N.F. Fragopanagos. "The Interaction of Attention and Emotion." *Neural Networks* 18 (2005): 353–369.

Wakatsuki, T., J. Schlessinger, and E.L. Elson. "The Biochemical Response of the Heart to Hypertension and Exercise. *Trends in Biochemical Sciences* 29 (2004): 609–617.

Weaver, A. J., and H.G. Koenig. "Religion, Spirituality, and Their Relevance to Medicine: An Update." *American Academy of Family Physicians* 73 (2006): 1336–1337. Available online. URL: *http://www.aafp.org/afp/20060415/editorials.html#e2*. Accessed on December 19, 2006.

Williams, R. J., and G. Deason. "Individuality in Vitamin C Needs." *Proceedings of the National Academy of Sciences, U S A* 57 (1967): 1638–1641. Available online. URL: *http://www.pubmedcentral.nih.gov/articlerender.fcgi?tool=pubmed&pubmedid=5231398*. Accessed on December 19, 2006.

Web Sites

Akil, H. A., and M. I. Morano. "Stress," American College of Neuropsychopharmacology. Available online. URL: *http://www.acnp.org/g4/GN401000073/CH073.html.*

American Chemical Society. "Scientists Say Vitamin C May Alleviate the Body's Response to Stress," *ScienceDaily.* Available online. URL: *http://www.sciencedaily.com/releases/1999/08/990823072615.htm.*

American Journal of Physiology. "Discovering the Role of the Adrenal Gland in the Control of Body Function." 2004. Available online. URL: *http://ajpregu.physiology.org/cgi/content/full/287/5/R1007#BIBL.*

American Heart Association. "Metabolic Syndrome," About.com. Available online. URL: *http://stress.about.com/gi/dynamic/offsite.htm?zi=1/XJ&sdn=stress&zu=http%3A%2F%2Fwww.americanheart.org%2Fpresenter.jhtml%3Fidentifier%3D534.*

Asthma.com. "The Basics of Asthma." Available online. URL: *http://www.asthma.com/the_basics_of_asthma.html.*

Boston University School of Medicine. "A Look at Centenarians," The New England Centenarian Study. Available online. URL: *http://www.bumc.bu.edu/Dept/Content.aspx?DepartmentID=361&PageID=5749.*

Bowen, R. "Glucocorticoids," Colorado State University. Available online. URL: *http://www.vivo.colostate.edu/hbooks/pathphys/endocrine/adrenal/gluco.html.*

Brehm, Barbara A. "Exercise and Stress," FitnessManagement.com. Available online. URL: *http://www.fitnessmanagement.com/FM/tmpl/genPage.asp?p=/information/articles/library/labnotes/labnotes896.html.*

Cherniss, Cary. "Emotional Intelligence: What It Is and Why It Matters," The Consortium for Research on Emotional Intelligence in Organizations. Available online. URL: *http://www.eiconsortium.org/research/what_is_emotional_intelligence.htm.*

Cleveland Plain Dealer. "Rosemary Kennedy, " Cleveland.com. Available online. URL: *http://www.legacy.net/Cleveland/LegacySubPage2.asp?Page=LifeStory&PersonID=3016806.*

Comeau, Sylvain. "Stress, Memory, and Social Support," *McGill Reporter*. Available online. URL: *http://www.mcgill.ca/ reporter/35/02/lupien/*.

Dahl, Stephan. "A Short Introduction to Nonverbal Behavior." Available online. URL: *http://stephan.dahl.at/nonverbal/non-verbal_ communication.html*.

Department of Health and Human Services. "Chronic Fatigue Syndrome: Basic Facts," Centers for Disease Control and Prevention (CDC). Available online. URL: *http://www.cdc.gov/cfs/cfsbasicfacts. htm#possiblecausescfs*.

Dubuc, Bruno. "The Amygdala and Its Allies," The Brain from Top to Bottom. Available online. URL: *http://thebrain.mcgill.ca/flash/i/i_04/ i_04_cr/i_04_cr_peu/i_04_cr_peu.html*.

Fogoros, Richard N. "Dysautonomia," About.com. Available online. URL: *http://heartdisease.about.com/cs/womensissues/a/ dysautonomia.htm*.

Fonorow, Owen R. "The Cure for Heart Disease: Condensed," Vitamin C Foundation. Available online. URL: *http://www. thecureforheartdisease.com/owen/HeartCureRD.htm*.

Gabriel, Gerald. "Hans Selye: The Discovery of Stress," Brain Connection. Available online. URL: *http://www.brainconnection.com/ topics/?main=fa/selye#A1*.

Hager, Joseph C. "Introduction to the DataFace Site: Facial Expressions, Emotion Expressions, Nonverbal Communication, Physiognomy," DataFace. Available online. URL: *http://face-and-emotion.com/ dataface/general/homepage.jsp*.

Harper, Jennifer. "Churchgoing Correlated to Longevity." *The Washington Times* (April 4, 2006). Available online. URL: *http://www. washtimes.com/national/20060403-103809-9183r.htm*.

Hewish, Paul. "Kluver-Bucy Syndrome," PatientPlus. Available online. URL: *http://www.patient.co.uk/showdoc/40001247/*.

Higdon, Jane. "Vitamin C," The Linus Pauling Institute. Available online. URL: *http://lpi.oregonstate.edu/infocenter/vitamins/ vitaminC/index.html*.

Hood, Craig S. "Endocrine Glands–Pituitary," Dr. Craig S. Hood, Professor of Biological Sciences, Loyola University New Orleans. Available online. URL: *http://www.loyno.edu/~chood/histnotesendo. html.*

Howard, Ken. "Do Brain Cells Regenerate?" *Princeton Weekly Bulletin* (April 5, 1999). Available online. URL: *http://www.princeton.edu/pr/ pwb/99/0405/brain.htm.*

Jameson, David. "Hypothalamic-Pituitary-Adrenal (HPA) Axis," Mind-Body-Health.net. Available online. URL: *http://www.mind-body-health.net/index.html?hpa.html&1.*

Kantrowitz, Mark. "Personal Space," eduPASS. Available online. URL: *http://www.edupass.org/culture/personalspace.phtml.*

Kimball, John W. "The Adrenal Glands," Kimball's Biology Pages. Available online. URL: *http://home.comcast.net/~john.kimball1/ BiologyPages/A/Adrenals.html.*

King, Michael W. "Steroid Hormones and Receptors," Indiana University School of Medicine, Medical Biochemistry page. Available online. URL: *http://web.indstate.edu/thcme/mwking/steroid-hormones. html.*

Klabunde, Richard E. "Cardiovascular Physiology Concepts," Cardiovascular Physiology Concepts. Available online. URL: *http://www.cvphysiology.com/index.html.*

———. "Circulating Catecholamines," Cardiovascular Physiology Concepts. Available online. URL: *http://www. cvphysiology.com/Blood%20Pressure/BP018.htm.*

Larsen, Hans R. "Vitamin C: Your Ultimate Health Insurance," International Health News. Available online. URL: *http://vvv.com/ healthnews/vitamin_C.html.*

Lehrer, Jonah. "The Reinvention of the Self: A Mind-Altering Idea Reveals How Life Affects the Brain," Seedmagazine.com. Available online. URL: *http://www.seedmagazine.com/news/2006/02/the_ reinvention_of_the_self.php?page=1.*

Lescouflair, Edric. "Walter Bradford Cannon: Experimental Physiologist," Harvard Square Library. Available online.

URL: *http://www.harvardsquarelibrary.org/unitarians/cannon_walter.html.*

Mayer, John D. "Emotional Intelligence Information." Available online. URL: *http://www.unh.edu/emotional_intelligence/.*

Mercola, Joseph. "Fish Oil Benefits the Heart and Brain." Available online. URL: *http://www.mercola.com/2003/sep/6/fish_oil.htm.*

National Institute on Alcohol Abuse and Alcoholism (NIAAA). "Alcohol: What You Don't Know Can Harm You." Available online. URL: *http://pubs.niaaa.nih.gov/publications/WhatUDontKnow_HTML/dontknow.htm.*

National Institute of Diabetes and Digestive and Kidney Diseases (NIDDK). "Cushing's Syndrome," The Endocrine and Metabolic Diseases Information Service. Available online. URL: *http://endocrine.niddk.nih.gov/pubs/cushings/cushings.htm.*

National Institute of Diabetes and Digestive and Kidney Diseases (NIDDK) Office of Health Research Reports. "Addison's Disease," The Endocrine and Metabolic Diseases Information Service. Available online. URL: *http://www.endocrine.niddk.nih.gov/pubs/addison/addison.htm.*

National Institute on Drug Abuse. "Studies Link Stress and Drug Addiction." Available online: URL: *http://www.nida.nih.gov/NIDA_Notes/NNVol14N1/Stress.html.*

Newhouse, Brian. "H. M.'s Brain and the History of Memory," NPR News. Available online. URL: http://www.npr.org/templates/story/story.php?storyId=7584970&ft=1&f=1024.

Nussey, Stephen, and Saffron Whitehead. "The Adrenal Gland," in: *Endocrinology: An Integrated Approach.* Available online. URL: *http://www.ncbi.nlm.nih.gov/books/bv.fcgi?rid=endocrin.chapter.442.*

Okinawa Centenarian Study. Available online. URL: *http://okinawaprogram.com/study.html.*

Persons, Susan M. "Social Support, Stress, and the Common Cold," Office of Behavioral and Social Sciences Research (OBSSR). Available online. URL: *http://obssr.od.nih.gov/Content/Publications/Articles/socsup.htm.*

Phelps, James R. "Exercise and Mood: Not the Usual Rap," Psycheducation.org. Available online. URL: *http://www.psycheducation.org/hormones/Insulin/exercise.htm.*

Psychology Today staff. "Vitamin C: Stress Buster," Psychology Today. Available online. URL: *http://www.psychologytoday.com/articles/pto-20030425-000001.html.*

Reh, Thomas A. "Neural Stem Cells: Form and Function." Available online. URL: *http://www.nature.com/neuro/journal/v5/n5/pdf/nn0502-392.pdf.*

Resource Library Magazine. "Women on the Verge: The Culture of Neurasthenia in 19th-Century America." Available online. URL: *http://www.tfaoi.com/aa/4aa/4aa463.htm.*

Salvatore, Steve. "Stressed out? Vitamin C is Possibly the Perfect Chill Pill, CNN.com. Available online. URL: *http://www.cnn.com/HEALTH/9908/23/vitaminc.stress.*

Sardi, Bill. "No More War Against Vitamin C," LewRockwell.com. Available online. URL: *http://www.lewrockwell.com/sardi/sardi33.html.*

Schaffhausen, Joanna. "The Strange Tale of Phineas Gage," Brain Connection. Available online. URL: *http://www.brainconnection.com/topics/?main=fa/phineas-gage.*

Selye, Hans. "The Nature of Stress," International Center for Nutritional Research. Available online. URL: *http://www.icnr.com/articles/thenatureofstress.html.*

Society for Neuroscience. "Bliss and the Brain," Society for Neuroscience. Available online. URL: *http://www.sfn.org/index.cfm?pagename=brainBriefings_blissAndTheBrain.*

Sparacino, Diane. "Lobotomy Was Once a Treatment for Mentally Ill," *San Bernardino Sun.* Available online. URL: *http://lang.sbsun.com/projects/lostamongus/displayarticle.asp?part=3&article=art04_lobotomy.*

Stone, Jeff. "Living to 100: Centenarians Show Us How," ThirdAge. Available online. URL: *http://www.thirdage.com/healthgate/files/13400.html.*

Swar, Mary, and John Kihlstrom. "Flashbulb Memories." Available online. URL: *http://socrates.berkeley.edu/~kihlstrm/wpa02flashbulb.htm.*

University of Dayton. "Walter Bradford Cannon." Available online. URL: *http://elvers.udayton.edu/history/people/Cannon.html.*

University of Massachusetts Neuroscience and Behavior Program. "Kluver-Bucy Syndrome." Available online. URL: *http://www-unix.oit.umass.edu/~gjdlab/Dar.html.*

Virginia Commonwealth University Department of Pathology. "Adrenal Pathology Lecture: Adrenal Overview and Pathologies." Available online. URL: *http://www.pathology.vcu.edu/education/endocrine/endocrine/adrenal/Index.htm.*

WebMD. "Immunoglobulins." Available online. URL: http://www.webmd.com/hw/lab_tests/hw41342.asp.

Further Reading

Books

Carper, Jean. *Your Miracle Brain.* New York: HarperCollins Publishers, 2000.

Cooper, Cary L. *Stress and Strain.* Oxford: Health Press, 1999.

Goleman, D. *Emotional Intelligence: Why It Can Matter More Than IQ.* New York: Bantam Books, 1995.

Matravers, D. *Art and Emotion.* Oxford: Clarendon Press, 1998.

McEwen, B. S., with E. N. Lasley. *The End of Stress As We Know It.* Washington, D.C.: Joseph Henry Press, 2002.

Talbott, S. M. *The Cortisol Connection: Why Stress Makes You Fat and Ruins Your Health—And What You Can Do About It.* Almeda, Calif.: Hunter House, 2002.

Web Sites

BrainSource.com
http://www.brainsource.com

Brain Web
http://www.dana.org/brainweb/

A Brief Introduction to the Brain
http://ifcsun1.ifisiol.unam.mx/Brain/segunda.htm

A Conversation with Bruce McEwen
http://www.brainconnection.com/topics/?main=conv/mcewen

Cortisol and Your Body
http://stress.about.com/od/stresshealth/a/cortisol.htm

Emotions
http://groups.msn.com/brainscience/emotions.msnw

Experiments Demonstrating the Amygdala's Role in Fear Conditioning
http://courses.umass.edu/psy391h/pathways.html

Glucocorticoids
http://www.reference.com/browse/wiki/Glucocorticoid

Hans Selye: The Discovery of Stress
http://www.brainconnection.com/topics/?main=fa/selye

The HOPES Brain Tutorial
http://www.stanford.edu/group/hopes/basics/braintut/ab1.html

How to Create Truly Supportive Friendships
http://stress.about.com/od/relationships/a/friendskills.htm

Linus Pauling—Scientist for the Ages
http://dwb.unl.edu/Teacher/NSF/C04/C04Links/osu.orst.edu/dept/lpi/lpbio/lpbio2.html

Neuroscience Education
http://faculty.washington.edu/chudler/ehceduc.html

Neuroscience Tutorial
http://thalamus.wustl.edu/course

Stress
http://groups.msn.com/BrainScience/stress.msnw

Stress and Disease: The Contributions of Hans Selye
to Neuroimmune Biology
http://home.cc.umanitoba.ca/~berczii/page2.htm

Stress and Drug Abuse
http://www.nida.nih.gov/Drugpages/Stress.html

Want to Live to Be 100?
http://www.readersdigest.ca/mag/2003/05/hundred.htm

Picture Credits

5: © WDCN/Univ. College
London/Photo Researchers, Inc.
12: © Infobase Publishing
14: © Infobase Publishing
15: © Infobase Publishing
22: © Infobase Publishing
23: © Infobase Publishing
26: © Infobase Publishing
28: © Infobase Publishing
30: © Infobase Publishing
35: © Infobase Publishing
39: © Infobase Publishing

40: © Infobase Publishing
45: © Infobase Publishing
46: © Infobase Publishing
52: © Infobase Publishing
58: © Infobase Publishing
61: © Infobase Publishing
64: © Infobase Publishing
68: © Infobase Publishing
75: © Infobase Publishing
80: © Infobase Publishing
87: © Infobase Publishing
89: © Infobase Publishing

Index

Brody, Stuart, 106
Browning, Elizabeth Barrett, 2
Brown, Roger, 56
Bucy, Paul, 43

Cahill, Larry, 57
Callaghan, Patrick, 99
Campbell, Samuel, 105–106
Cannon, Walter
    research of, 14–15, 60, 62
Cannon-Bard theory, 15
Cardiovascular system
    and disease, 74, 76, 82–83, 96–98, 100,
        102, 104, 106–108
    and exercise, 97–98
    and stress, 73–74, 76, 82–83, 105
Catecholamine
    effects of, 73
    receptors, 74
Cell body, 21, 44
Central nervous system
    components, 24, 65, 69
Cerebellum, 25
    functions, 14, 27
Cerebral cortex,
    functions, 29–30
    gyri, 27, 29, 50–51, 86
    lobes of, 27–28
    sulci, 27–28
Cerebral hemispheres
    structures in, 25–27, 29, 49
Cerebral ventricles, 26
Cerebrospinal fluid (CSF), 26
Chronic fatigue syndrome, 7
    causes, 71
    symptoms, 70
Classical conditioning, 88
Clearne, Anthony, 71
Cognitive functions
    and emotions, 8, 10–11, 38, 49–51,
        53
Cohen, Sheldon, 83
Collagen synthesis, 103–104
Conditioned emotional response
    fear, 51–53
Conscious thoughts
    control of, 39, 49
    influences of, 6
Corpus callosum, 25, 30
Corticotrophin-releasing hormone
    production of, 66–67, 71, 79, 85
    and withdrawal, 95

Cortisol
    effects of, 67–69, 73–74, 76, 78–79, 81–82,
        86–87
    feedback control of, 66–67, 86
    high levels of, 71–72, 90, 105
    low levels of, 69–72, 78
    receptors, 67
    release of, 66, 106
    and the secretion of insulin, 67–68, 76
Cushing's syndrome (Hypercortisolism)
    causes, 72, 87
    symptoms, 71–72
    treatment, 72, 90–91

Daydreaming, 10, 38
Deason, Gary, 104–105
Dendrites
    functions, 21
    remodeling, 86–87
    spines, 21
    tree, 21, 86, 90–91
Depression
    and stress, 83, 91–93, 108
    treatment, 35, 99
Dhabhar, Firdaus, 81
Diabetes
    prevention, 96–97
    type 1, 84
    type 2, 76, 97
Diurnal rhythm, 66
Diencephalon, 25, 27
Digestive system, 77–78
Disgust or dislike, 4
    and interpersonal space, 18–19
    responses, 6
Dolan, Raymond, 54
Dopamine, 23
    and addiction, 94
    release of, 42, 44, 81, 91, 94
Dorsal prefrontal cortex, 31
Duchenne smile, 13
Dysautonomia, 7

Ectopic ACTH syndrome, 72
EEG. See Electroencephalogram
Ekman, Paul
    research of, 3–4, 11, 13
Electroencephalogram (EEG), 36, 98
Electrophysiological techniques, 36–37
Emotion
    and art, 2–3
    and attention, 53–55

About the Author

F. Fay Evans-Martin, Ph.D., has a dual background in the areas of pharmacology and biopsychology. Her degrees include a B.S. with a major in biology from Georgia Southern University, an M.S. in pharmacology from the Medical College of Georgia, and a Ph.D. in psychology from the University of Georgia. Her postdoctoral research includes spinal cord injury research at the University of Alabama and nicotine self-administration research at the University of Pittsburgh. Dr. Evans-Martin has also taught undergraduate psychology courses, most recently at the University of Louisville. She is the mother of two sons, Shawn and Eric.

About the Editor

Eric H. Chudler, Ph.D., is a research neuroscientist who has investigated the brain mechanisms of pain and nociception since 1978. Dr. Chudler received his Ph.D. from the Department of Psychology at the University of Washington in Seattle. He has worked at the National Institutes of Health and directed a laboratory in the neurosurgery department at Massachusetts General Hospital. Between 1991 and 2006, Dr. Chudler was a faculty member in the Department of Anesthesiology at the University of Washington. He is currently a research associate professor in the University of Washington Department of Bioengineering and director of education and outreach at University of Washington Engineered Biomaterials.